Tonkin Zulaikha Greer Architects

Editor: Patrick Bingham-Hall
Design: Stephen Smedley

Pesaro Publishing

PO Box 74
Balmain NSW 2041
Australia
Phone 61 2 9555 7422
Fax 61 2 9818 6999
Email pesaro@bigpond.net.au

First Published in 2005 by Pesaro Publishing, Sydney, Australia

London, Geoffrey.

Tonkin Zulaikha Greer.

Bibliography.

Includes index.

ISBN 1 877015 07 5.

Tonkin Zulaikha Greer (Firm).

Architecture, Modern - Australia.
I. Bingham-Hall, Patrick. II. Title.
(Series: Pesaro monograph series).

720.994

Tonkin Zulaikha Greer Architects

Contents

right
Olympic Plaza Lighting
Towers,
2000.

following page
The Australian War
Memorial, London,
2003
with Janet Laurence, artist.

Adrian Dannatt

Freighted with danger

I am well aware that there is a vast discourse, an entire library, ranging from the highly theoretical nay philosophical to the altogether practical, concerning the question of 'Australian architecture.' The question, of course, being whether there is indeed such a thing, how it would be identifiable and specifically differentiated from other forms of building in other countries. There is even, I fear, a tighter debate as to differences between architecture in specific Australian cities, notably between Sydney and that other metropolis further south, namely Melbourne, a debate doubtless freighted with danger.

On all above issues I happily plead innocence and might ignorantly add that I am not sure I always think of Tonkin Zulaikha Greer as 'Australian architects' as opposed to architects who live and work much of the time in Australia. What I am confident about is the dexterity, intelligence and delight in their built work and, though some might ascribe this to their being based in Australia or Sydney, I personally suspect it is due to their own abilities. But perhaps it could be claimed that at this sheer distance, both geographical and psychological, from the fixed battles of architectural history, it would be ridiculous to believe in the certainty of only one dominant aesthetic. This allows TZG an enviable freedom and openness, a clarity from remove, in which a variety of interesting opportunities are all simultaneously in play, the epitome of that culture of 'both/and' rather than 'either/or'.

TZG are unusual as a practice because they seem to be able to operate as all architects would wish, outside the definitions and limitations inevitably imposed by the eventual workday realities of the business. They are not a 'big'

Brian Zulaikha, Tim Greer
and Peter Tonkin.

practice nor a small one, but a perfectly sized, impeccably structured office that fit into their actual studio space with a pleasing rightness. They could never be termed a 'commercial' firm, indeed the atmosphere of the office is as far as one could get from those massive American-style architectural machines, yet they work on major commercial developments. From a background in public government projects the firm has become increasingly involved in profitable projects for large scale developers. This makes TZG the opposite of those bijou 'creative' bureaux known only for residential conversions, restaurants and 'loft style' accommodation, but at the same time some of their most memorable work has been of this genre. Without making a great fuss about it, TZG create architectonic solutions to specific demands, whereby the process of the project becomes the project itself. Thus they somehow manage to be fully attentive to the clients in the manner of any mainstream practice whilst maintaining an unusual aesthetic freedom. The sheer range of their work and their refusal of any trademark 'house style' is proof of a flexibility, creative and practical, all too rare today.

It may be unfashionable to link architecture and its authors, the preferred myth being of an autonomous process that emerges almost without human agency, but I would ride this taboo by suggesting that, whilst acknowledging the inestimable contributions of all the staff members, the sophisticated fluency of TZG is at least partly due to the character of its three partners. After all there must be some generational significance to the neat spread of ages between Brian Zulaikha at 60, Peter Tonkin at 50 and Tim Greer at 40, a range which guarantees the richest possible mixture of references, influences and results. Indeed the

extra-ordinary openness, the sheer optimistic energy of the partners must come from the daily interaction of their differing background, and their seemingly unquenchable curiosity and engagement with all forms of building.

Thus, whilst too many architects complain about this or are deeply opposed to that, see themselves as surrounded by hostile forces or rival systems, all three TZG partners seem equally positive about everything, without a bad word to say about anyone else. Without wishing to cast them as Candide, there is a lack of cynicism, an absolute lack of bitterness or professional paranoia about Tonkin, Zulaikha and Greer, which is not only restoratively refreshing but overt in the work they make. For as with Warhol there is a power to 'liking things' far greater than the negativity of constant criticism, if you truly love the world around you and actively enjoy its cultural fabric it is natural to then contribute to it oneself. This is the optimism referred to by JJP Oud when he announced "If I were not an optimist I could not be an architect", a belief in the still achievable best.

The character, the personal nature, of an architect is something that is forbidden to be mentioned in any analysis of their work, even if it directly affects the running of their office, until they are considered worthy of an actual biography or documentary film. And at that point they nearly always turn out to have been egotistical monsters. Thus though the biographical is strictly verboten, one might break this rule to say that there are very, very few architects as highly successful as TZG who are also pleasant, amusing, modest, considerate and yes, just 'nice' people. And surely these seemingly irrelevant characteristics do determine their daily practice, their projects. Tonkin, Zulaikha and

Greer are highly intellectual, well-read, widely-traveled architects who have seemingly visited each necessary building all over the world and read every book required, but they never use this as an excuse or alibi for their actual work, resisting the faintest hint of pomposity.

If Zulaikha might be cast as the group's senior International Style soi-disant 'Brutalist', Tonkin would play the eclectic po-modernist, once influenced by the vernacular ideas of Venturi, and Greer could represent that pro-modernist generation emerging from the other end of the 1980s. But the reality is naturally far more complex, more shaded. For though Zulaikha certainly demonstrates an unusual affection for some much maligned buildings, always willing to see the best side of any structure, Tonkin is equally passionate in his knowledge of historic Australian architecture (apparently knowing the smallest detail of every building in Sydney) whilst Greer casts a wry eye over the myriad models available. Yet all three of them are united in a sheer practicality, a physical involvement with the tangible building process. This becomingly modest 'truth to materials' allows them to be up a ladder fixing a window detail in their own kitchen whilst developing a multi-million dollar master scheme.

Tonkin, as historic regional expert and indeed a practicing archeologist, worked with Zulaikha on the reconstruction of Hyde Park Barracks Museum, an archeological revelation of every layer of that building's history, including the most recent ones. This was an entirely successful demonstration that architecture can never be static or permanent, a project with its own, literal, in-built expendability. As such, with its 'Ghost Stair' and 'Void' it could be compared to

subsequent work by Libeskind, like the Jewish Museum and his scheme for the former SS barracks at Sachsenhausen as well as Cedric Price's theories of temporality. Hyde Park Barracks proves an altogether radical new approach to 'heritage' conservation not yet rivaled elsewhere. It might also be compared to the work of artists, such as Robert Smithson's industrial-archeology or Lara Almarcegui's 'Extracting the Cement from the Façade', doing just that to a municipal building in Brussels in 1999 or her painstaking restoration of the market of Gros in Spain the very day before its demolition.

For TZG have a vital interest in the visual arts, and these collaborations or potential parallels can be seen in many of their projects. Sometimes this 'artistic' element is overt, as at their war memorials, but even Tonkin's own house — built on an impossibly thin and seemingly valueless site — recalls the work of Gordon Matta-Clark. Specifically, when he went round the boroughs of New York buying narrow empty lots from the city, overlooked corners of land nobody else wanted, and staking them out as art works. The use of Cor-Ten for the Hume Freeway may echo the sculptural dramatics of Richard Serra or even Christo, but it also fits perfectly with the landscape. The lighting pylons at the Olympic Plaza operate as highly efficient independent units and do not hide their overt functionality, yet at the same time they manage to reference the heroic revolutionary design of Russian Constructivism. Likewise the twisted-twin houses Greer designed at Bondi Beach not only reference Lutyens, Bruce Goff and Arts & Craft interiors but they also could be compared to Dan Graham's mirrored pavilions, Schwitter's Merzbau or the 'uncanny' dopplegangers of the young artist Gregor Schneider.

But thankfully none of these three architects would dream of making such comparisons themselves, indeed might blushingly deny them, as they wear their art-world knowledge pleasingly lightly. For all their buildings have **architectural** meaning rather than other meanings, a complexity of program and execution, a personal involvement, that distinguishes them from the routine work all too often produced by firms regardless of reputation. This urge to make 'good' buildings, interesting buildings, at whatever the obligation, even when not actually necessary, is what defines the oeuvre of TZG. Their buildings are always "better than they need to be" as they put the same amount of attention and intelligence into the most commercial developer-led project as they do into their own homes or a friend's studio. One might even dare use the term 'love' for the devotion TZG give to every project, even when only half of such energy is actually required by the clients, when many other architects would adjust the level of their involvement down to meet the bare limits of the brief. It is this fundamental pride, the pride of making architecture and not just building, that is so often squeezed out of equivalent practices elsewhere by the sheer and increasing cruelty of the game.

This lack of meanness, the generosity of Tonkin Zulaikha Greer is as clear in their projects as in their daily discourse. They make a 'gift' of a series of blue tile water pools and rich limestone rock walls for the Pavilions on the Bay complex. Unasked for, they always generously give to every space more than is required or expected. In terms of such materiality TZG play with code and expectations, using blue glaze tile and yellow balconies that suggest a modernist North European working-class housing project for a luxury condo development. It is this sense of architecture as an exchange, of trust and abundance, a generosity akin to Potlach that distinguishes the work of Tonkin Zulaikha Greer from the literal 'meanness', of materials and spirit, of so much building today. Not to see what they can get away with, but to see what is the very best they could achieve, but really the very best, on every single occasion. As such their practice proudly recalls those words of Francis Greenway, writing on public works back in 1814 "An elegant & classical pile of building may often be carried into effect by an able architect possessing integrity for a less sum of money than the meanest production of pretenders whose only object is to gain as much as they can by those who are weak enough to trust them."

Geoffrey London

Tonkin Zulaikha Greer Architects

Tonkin Zulaikha Greer signify architectural practice in early 21st Century Australia. There is immense respect for and knowledge of Sydney, their city of operation, and a desire and expectation to create a great urban model. They have a reflective, self-critical attitude to their own work and its place in the city; an understanding of the value of working with existing built fabric and the cultural values it embodies; a constant desire to be contemporary in their formal solutions and the issues they embrace; a willingness to be experimental and to take each project on its own merits; and a profound respect for the discipline of architecture.

There is also a truly catholic breadth to the practice's professional interests and capacities. Although the practice regards itself as operating without a consistent aesthetic approach,[1] there are, nonetheless, recurring themes that result in a recognisably coherent community of buildings.

The process of construction, the art of building made manifest, significantly determines the aesthetic of their work. Elements are brought together in such a way as to maximise their delineation and articulation. Adjacency and collage are more important than seamless junctions.

Tonkin Zulaikha Greer use what they call 'real' materials, materials with thickness, depth and volume rather than the thin-ness of applied surfaces. This interest lends a robustness to their buildings and is a part of the practice's preoccupation with the experiential qualities of design.

Experiences are generated by contact with the real materials, the reality of the forms defining spaces, the careful control of natural light and the modulation of spatial experiences.

Tonkin Zulaikha Greer rank the experiential as more important than the highly resolved architectural object.Their attitude to materials reflects an allegiance to a version of architectural Modernism filtered through the perceptions and ethics of Alison and Peter Smithson. The Smithsons developed the term 'New Brutalism' in the 1950s as a way of describing an architecture of rigour and social commitment. They called for an awareness of the modern architect's moral responsibilities and demanded a direct involvement with building materials and their qualities. This, they insisted, would result in an ethically supportable building. The Smithsons argued, (in opposition to Reyner Banham's view of New Brutalism as a movement characterised by raw concrete and exposed brickwork)[2]

Brutalist to us meant 'Direct' – to others it came to be a synonym for rough, crude, oversized, concrete and using beams three times thicker than necessary. Brutalism was opposite.[3]

The term 'Brutalist' has been applied to the work of Tonkin Zulaikha Greer[4] and the attributes promoted by the Smithsons are evident in their architecture.

Traces of formal references to the Russian Constructivism of the early 20th Century can be seen throughout their work, but this also has an ideological base. The work of the Constructivists was committed to the newly established collective, of which the public realm was a physical embodiment. Tonkin Zulaikha Greer refer to the architecture representing this aspiration when developing their own propositions for the public realm.

For Tonkin Zulaikha Greer, the ethic of architectural practice in the early 21st Century also includes the application of environmentally sustainable design principles; an attitude to old and disused buildings that recognises their role in a city and encourages their return to active use; a foregrounding and exposure of the process rather than the refined object; and the provision of architectural services across a broad spectrum of client types. These themes can be traced through the history of the practice.

Beginnings

The practice has its roots in 1977, when Brian Zulaikha and Peter Tonkin worked together in the New South Wales Government Architect's Office. They came together again in 1984 after Peter Tonkin, then working with Lawrence Nield & Partners, won an ideas competition for renovating the Overseas Passenger Terminal on Circular Quay. Brian Zulaikha had also left the Government Architect's Office but was invited by them to return and coordinate the re-design of the Circular Quay public domain.^

Tonkin's idea for the spectacular site opposite the Sydney Opera House was to create a new public waterfront space. The Terminal's concrete cladding was removed and the new glass skin revealed its industrial skeleton, the original bones of the building, transforming what had been a solid impenetrable lump into a new transparent and publicly accessible jewel. A dormant part of the Quay was reactivated and major new urban spaces were created. The dynamic exposure of structure, escalators, decks and walkways, all dramatically rendered in orange, showed an interest in a type of expressive functionalism related to the Constructivist source of the architectural

A. IN JULY 1993, THE NSW DEPT OF PUBLIC WORKS AND THE NSW PRESIDENT, OF THE RAIA, CHRIS JOHNSON, HELD AN 'IDEAS COMPETITION' FOR THE LARGE AND UNDERUSED 1960 OVERSEAS PASSENGER TERMINAL. A WINNING ENTRY BY PETER TONKIN, WHICH PROPOSED THE DEMOLITION OF A THIRD OF THE BUILDING TO CREATE A NEW WATERFRONT 'PIAZZETTA', AND THE REMOVAL OF ITS BLANK CONCRETE CLADDING TO EXPOSE ITS DYNAMIC STEEL FRAME, CAUGHT THE ATTENTION OF THE PREMIER OF NSW. THIS LED TO TONKIN BEING ENGAGED, WITH HIS THEN EMPLOYER, LAWRENCE NIELD AND PARTNERS, TO UNDERTAKE THE REFURBISHMENT OF THE BUILDING AND THE DESIGN OF THE ADJOINING NEW WATERFRONT OPEN SPACE. THE TERMINAL WORK WAS PART OF A SIGNIFICANT CIVIC IMPROVEMENT PROGRAM TO OPEN UP CIRCULAR QUAY FOR THE 1988 BICENTENNIAL OF WHITE SETTLEMENT, MANAGED BY BRIAN ZULAIKHA IN THE DEPT OF PUBLIC WORKS. THE BUILDING WAS COMPLETED IN 1987.

A SUBSEQUENT DECLINE IN SHIPPING ACTIVITY ALLOWED A FURTHER REDUCTION IN THE PORT USE OF THE BUILDING, AND THE INSERTION OF A LARGE AMOUNT OF RETAIL SPACE INTO THE VACATED PARTS. THE NEW PROJECT (COMPLETED IN 2002 NOT BY TZG), INVOLVED THE REMOVAL OF MUCH OF THE 1987 WORK, PARTICULARLY AT THE SOUTHERN END OF THE BUILDING.

Peter Tonkin's entry for the Overseas Passenger Terminal Ideas Competition, 1983.

B. THE PRACTICE COMMENCED AS TONKIN ZULAIKHA ARCHITECTS. BYRON HARFORD, WHO WAS BORN IN AUCKLAND, NEW ZEALAND AND STUDIED AT THE UNIVERSITY OF TECHNOLOGY, SYDNEY, JOINED TONKIN ZULAIKHA ARCHITECTS IN 1988 AND THE PRACTICE CHANGED ITS NAME TO TONKIN ZULAIKHA HARFORD IN SEPTEMBER 1992, FOLLOWING HIS APPOINTMENT AS A DIRECTOR. HE RESIGNED FROM THE PRACTICE AT THE BEGINNING OF 1994 AND THE COMPANY CHANGED ITS NAME BACK TO TONKIN ZULAIKHA ARCHITECTS. BYRON HARFORD NOW HAS AN INDEPENDENT ARCHITECTURAL PRACTICE.

C. THE AUSTRALIAN COMMITTEE OF THE INTERNATIONAL COUNCIL ON MONUMENTS AND SITES (ICOMOS) MET IN THE SOUTH AUSTRALIAN TOWN OF BURRA IN 1979 TO FORMALIZE AN APPROACH TO THE CONSERVATION OF BUILDINGS. THIS LED TO THE ACCEPTANCE OF THE SO-CALLED BURRA CHARTER IN 1981 AS A BASIS FOR CONSERVATION PLANNING. ITS PRINCIPLES INCLUDE BASING DESIGN DECISIONS ON A SOUND UNDERSTANDING OF THE PLACE AND ITS SIGNIFICANCE, AND AN AVOIDANCE OF IMITATING HISTORICAL DETAIL.

imagery. There is a further interest evident in technique and in materials, with their particular qualities and their junctions being a major component of the architectural expression.

Zulaikha's work on the waterfront public domain resulted in a similarly successful civic outcome. A broad new edge was built around Circular Quay, stitching together different spaces and functions into a coherent new urban space. As with the Terminal, the selection of materials and detailing form a particularly important part of the coherence and expression of the space: no-nonsense, solid and durable, with full consideration given to the issue of appropriateness. In 1987, there was an acknowledgement that their shared approach would enable the two architects to form their own practice.

After several smaller projects, the Library Services Building (completed in 1991 for the Royal Blind Society of NSW) became the practice's 'breakthrough' job. This was a complex public building, although with a limited budget, and involved the insertion of a substantial complementary link between existing buildings. The new building accommodates the braille and talking book services together with associated production and other technical facilities.

Light, colour, sound, and texture are used in the design as internal guides for the partly sighted. These are manipulated by strategically placed openings and the careful selection of materials with differing resonances and surfaces, signaling different functions within the building. In this innovative way the interior is made perceptible and useable for those with severe visual impairment.

Externally, the building assumes an institutional distinctiveness through the formal strategy of applying separately articulated layers to the basic building block, the over-scaled roof drainage, the sun louvre system, and the protruding escape stair towers clad in red fibre-cement panels. The constituent parts of the construction and their mode of assembly are utilised as the major expressive device for the building. It was during this project that Tim Greer joined Tonkin and Zulaikha, later to become a partner. The building won a Merit Award from the NSW Chapter of the Royal Australian Institute of Architects (RAIA), bringing attention to the young practice.[B]

Transformations

The Hyde Park Barracks refurbishment in central Sydney reinforced both the attention and the architectural approach. Designed by the colonial architect Francis Greenway in 1817, its renovation by Tonkin Zulaikha in 1993 demonstrated how, while working within the rigorous constraints of the Burra Charter, it was possible to retain and enhance an understanding of the historical circumstances of the original building while allowing a radical insertion of new elements.[C]

It marked a philosophical shift in Australia for the heritage movement.

Enlightened clients[5], who had appreciated the use of steel and glass in the Overseas Passenger Terminal, wanted to see these materials used to define the new insertions into the Hyde Park Barracks. This distinctive approach marked a strong contrast to the building's original hand-wrought bricks and timber. Instead of full restoration and replication, the architects peeled away the accretions of nearly two hundred years to reveal the different layers of occupancy and the full history of the building over time, from convict barracks to immigration depot to female asylum and law courts before falling into disuse. Tonkin Zulaikha stabilised the decay of the Barracks and, with the insertion of substantial new black steel and glass display cases, converted it into a flourishing contemporary museum exposing the social and cultural history of the early period of Sydney's European settlement as well as the history of the building itself. The Hyde Park Barracks project was marked by a defiant lack of resolution, a rawness in finish and materials, and a willing acceptance of the aesthetic to which such an approach gives rise. It provided the opportunity in the arrangement of museum displays to develop a suite of designed objects, reminiscent of Carlo Scarpa's steel museum insertions but here systematised into repeatable, visually linked objects, a precursor for the work by Tonkin Zulaikha Greer at the Homebush Olympic Games site some years later.

Through the articulation of the new from the old, the project encouraged the definition of elements as separate and layered, a visual clarification of assembly and production.

The conversion of the Hyde Park Barracks won state and national RAIA Design Awards.

This project was a kind of laboratory for Tonkin Zulaikha, not only as a training ground for their subsequent work with heritage buildings but also as a means of testing and refining their major architectural strategies for the adaptive re-use and restoration of colonial buildings in Australia.

The Casula Powerhouse was a vast decommissioned electrical power station near Liverpool, on the outskirts of Sydney. A plebiscite to decide a new use for the heritage-listed building was held among the local ratepayers: ethnically diverse and, in the main, economically poor. Proposals for a council depot or a sports centre were rejected in favour of a cultural centre. On the strength of their work at the Hyde Park Barracks, Tonkin Zulaikha Greer were invited to participate in a limited architectural competition run by the Liverpool City Council. While the building was bought for a small net cost, a significant part of the modest renovation budget was spent in bringing drainage and power to the building, leaving very little money for a substantial internal makeover. However, on winning the project, the architects stitched through modest modifications carefully tailored for community needs which were determined after extensive consultation.

Tonkin Zulaikha Greer's design allowed for ongoing incremental changes and resulted in a most accessible and successful arts facility, a mix of exhibition galleries, production studios, performance spaces and artist-in-residence facilities. A range of significant Australian artists were commissioned to work with them in transforming the building, signalling its new use. The art works were allowed to become permanent fixtures within the building: the Turbine Hall, refitted as the major performance space, has a pigment stained floor painted by Judy Watson, while the vast openings facing west have been dramatically converted into giant fingerprint windows by Sydney installation artist Robyn Backen. [D & E]

Sydney's imperious Customs House facing Circular Quay, originally designed in the Greek

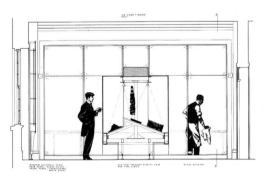

Hyde Park Barracks. Section of the Archaeology Room showcase, from the selection competition, 1989.

F. TZG JOINED WITH THE SYDNEY PRACTICE JACKSON TEECE CHESTERMAN WILLIS TO BID FOR THE CUSTOMS HOUSE PROJECT. TZG AND JTCW JOINTLY STAFFED A PROJECT-SPECIFIC ARCHITECTURAL OFFICE SET UP WITHIN THE VACATED CUSTOMS HOUSE, WITH PETER TONKIN AS DESIGN DIRECTOR AND DAVID JACKSON AS PRODUCTION DIRECTOR. JACKSON TEECE CHESTERMAN WILLIS DOCUMENTED THE EXTERNAL STONEWORK CONSERVATION.

G. IN 2002, THE FAILURE OF THE SYDNEY CITY COUNCIL TO FIND APPROPRIATE COMMERCIAL TENANTS FOR SOME AREAS IN THE CUSTOMS HOUSE LED TO A DECISION TO REWORK THE INTERIOR TO ACCOMMODATE TWO LEVELS OF COMMERCIAL OFFICE SPACE AND THE CITY OF SYDNEY LIBRARY. A DISPUTE ABOUT THE REMOVAL OF SIGNIFICANT HERITAGE FABRIC RESULTED IN THE PROJECT BEING DESIGNED BY OTHER ARCHITECTS, WHOSE PROPOSAL INCLUDES THE PARTIAL ENCLOSURE OF THE ATRIUM AND THE REMOVAL OF INTERIOR ELEMENTS DESIGNED BY TZG, SUCH AS THE LINKED STAIR AND ESCALATOR SYSTEM.

Revival manner by colonial architect Mortimer Lewis in 1843, has had a series of major additions and refurbishments by significant Sydney architects over the last 150 years. The building expanded with the growth of customs operations until, in 1990, the Federal Government made a 60-year gift of the building to Sydney City Council. With the building came money for its renovation, and the requirement that new uses, although not defined, be essentially public. An ideas-based competition was conducted and was won by Tonkin Zulaikha Greer with Sydney architects Jackson Teece Chesterman Willis.[F]

The winning design enabled a clear definition of the old from the new by preserving the most significant parts of the building, while allowing a high level of invention and substantial alteration to less important sections. The original U-shaped building had its courtyard filled with additions during World War 1. In the Tonkin Zulaikha Greer scheme, the courtyard was returned in the form of an inserted five-storey high atrium space with a steel and glass southern wall, against which the building's new escalators trace their diagonal patterns. Glass, as a contrasting material to the original stone building, was chosen to confirm the identity of the new insertion.

In light of the directive that the building is predominantly for public use, Tonkin Zulaikha Greer recognised the need to shift the perception of the building from one of forbidding authority to an open and inviting publicly-accessible facility. They achieved this by creating a new urban space that flows from the forecourt on Alfred Street, with its paving patterned by lines marking the shifting location of successive shorelines, 'the crashing of waves', into the atrium. The forecourt acts as an invitation leading into the space of the atrium.[G]

As with all the practice's adaptive re-use projects, the new architecture in Customs House is robust and well-defined, growing out of the strengths and constraints of the existing building but adding a distinctive and contemporary layer, contributing resolutely to the historical evolution of the building and the city. Tonkin Zulaikha Greer have a clear view of their role in the historical evolution arising from a close understanding of both architectural and Australian history. This serves the practice well in renovation projects for culturally important buildings.

Complementing their work on historically important building refurbishments, Tonkin Zulaikha Greer have become highly skilled at converting less distinguished existing buildings for new and appropriate commercial uses. They have undertaken several successful projects, such as the Norton Street and Verona cinema complexes, that have valued the existing urban fabric and have contributed to the communities surrounding them.

Sydney Customs House.
Concept section sketch
from the bid submission,
1994.

The Verona Cinema Complex is located on a corner of Sydney's Oxford Street. The utilitarian two-storey industrial brick building, once housing a paper factory, has been converted into a mixed-use development containing, in addition to four cinemas built on the roof, a cafe, a yoga centre, shops and a penthouse. The building both takes from and contributes to its location, establishing a new set of urban functions, both civic and commercial, that add another layer to the consistently evolving urban village of Paddington.

The client, who had purchased the disused factory, appointed the architects when no clear adaptive re-use strategy had been proposed. Tonkin Zulaikha Greer, supported by the knowledge that the building was designed to carry heavy loads and would not need structural reinforcing, devised the idea of placing cinemas on the roof, as individually expressed boxes discrete from the form of the existing building. The new forms of the development are clad in various metal sheetings, tough and resilient materials in response to the building's industrial past. With more than a nod towards the agit-prop function which the Constructivists gave to their designs for buildings serving the community, the stair well continues vertically to form an extended, naturally lit, framed lantern serving externally as a sign to the street. This proclaims, amidst the efflorescence of the added rooftop forms, the dynamism of the building's new uses.

The Norton Street Cinemas follow the precedent of the Verona, animating this precinct of the Italian enclave of Leichhardt with a variety of new day- and night-time uses. As with Verona, where the building to be developed has little architectural merit or historical interest, the design additions assume a more independent character, more forceful, and less dependent on the existing forms. Directed by the limits of the budget, the architectural elements are parked within the existing volume as autonomous forms containing autonomous functions. The four cinemas are compressed into the rear of the former 1970s tile warehouse, and are served by a single ceremonial access corridor.

The Constructivist imagery of the Verona street facade gets a further working here, with the cinema signage and light blades applied as hovering elemental fragments to the facade, thin and visually dynamic.

The recurring visual theme of the Norton Street Cinemas is light; light as projected through film in the cinemas, light as drama, light as the vehicle for creating transparency, and illusion and light as the means for transforming the building through the use of illuminated wall planes. The outcome is one of

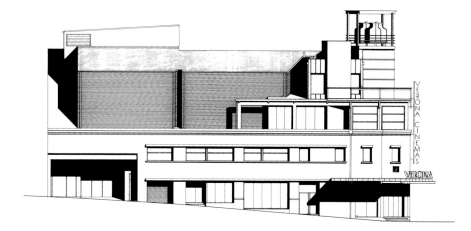

The Verona Cinemas.
Design drawing,
1994.

H. THE NATIONAL GALLERY OF AUSTRALIA PROJECT
(2000-2003) ILLUSTRATES THE CONUNDRUM OF
RESOLVING THE NEEDS OF EXISTING AND NEW
ARCHITECTURE.

TONKIN ZULAIKHA GREER WERE PLACED IN A
DIFFICULT POSITION – BETWEEN THE ROCK OF THE
CLIENT'S GENUINE NEEDS, AND THE HARD PLACE OF AN
ICON OF MODERN ARCHITECTURE. THE ISSUE CONCERNED
THE MORAL RIGHTS OF THE ORIGINAL ARCHITECT, COL
MADIGAN OF EDWARDS MADIGAN TORZILLO AND BRIGGS,
AND THE PERCEIVED SHORTCOMINGS OF THE 1970S
DESIGN. COMMONWEALTH LEGISLATION PROTECTING
MORAL RIGHTS WAS INTRODUCED HALF-WAY THROUGH
THE PROJECT'S DESIGN, AND FORMED THE BASIS FOR
COL MADIGAN'S OBJECTIONS TO THE BUILDING BEING
ALTERED.

TZG WON THE SELECTION COMPETITION ON THE BASIS
OF THEIR SENSITIVE TREATMENT OF THE EXISTING
BUILDING AND A DEMONSTRATED UNDERSTANDING OF ITS
PERCEIVED SHORTCOMINGS, AS WELL AS THEIR RESPECT
FOR MADIGAN'S HIGHLY PERSONAL ARCHITECTURE. TZG'S
TRACK RECORD OF SUCCESSFUL REWORKING OF HERITAGE
BUILDINGS FOR CONTEMPORARY CULTURAL USE
UNDERLAID THEIR APPROACH TO THE NGA PROJECT.

AS AN ESSENTIAL PART OF THE DESIGN WORK, TZG
SOUGHT DIALOGUE WITH COL MADIGAN AND DEEPLY
RESEARCHED THE ORIGINAL DESIGN. CHANGED VALUES
FROM 1969 TO 2001 MEAN THAT TZG'S PROPOSAL FOR
ALTERATION DIFFERED SIGNIFICANTLY FROM THAT OF COL
MADIGAN. DISCUSSIONS WITH MADIGAN WERE CONFINED
TO GENERAL STATEMENTS OF DESIGN PRINCIPLE, WHICH,
FOR MOST OF THE PROCESS, HE ACCEPTED. ON THE DESIGN
BEING RELEASED, OPPOSITION WAS SUSTAINED, AND
SUBSEQUENT NEGOTIATIONS LED TO ALTERNATIVE
PROPOSALS (SCHEMES B TO H) WHICH HAD LESS EFFECT
ON SIGNIFICANT PARTS OF THE BUILDING.

BY 2003, THE PROLONGED DESIGN PROCESS HAD
STALLED, AND TZG AND THE GALLERY AGREED TO
TERMINATE THE COMMISSION. THE WORK COMPLETED
WAS LIMITED TO A THOROUGH REFURBISHMENT OF THE
SERVICES AND GALLERY INTERIORS. BY 2004, ALTERNATIVE
ARCHITECTS WERE BEING SOUGHT BY THE GALLERY FOR A
REDUCED PROJECT.

"NGA Burns". Painting
by Neil Mackenzie,
2003.

**formal irresolution, an incomplete picture, in
keeping with the architects' recognition of the
evolutionary nature of buildings and the city:
just one layer in an ongoing layering of uses.**

The complexity of working with existing
buildings for refurbishment projects inevitably
carries a higher level of difficulty than other
architectural jobs. For Tonkin Zulaikha Greer
this has not been an issue, with the notable and
harrowing exception of the National Gallery of
Australia in Canberra. This was another project
won in competition, and the architects have
carried out part of the project only – important
internal work directed toward re-exposing the
architectural intentions of the original building,
a superbly finished concrete masterwork from
the 1960s, only completed in 1984.

In response to numerous additions made during
the life of the Gallery, they have reinstated many
of the original interiors, opening up views
from gallery to gallery, shrinking back applied
plaster wall panels to allow the concrete
architecture to be visible once again, removing
dropped ceilings to restore the monumental
volumes of the original building, lowering walls
back below the ceiling level to allow the
continuous ceiling planes to be visible, and re-
exposing fins and other key structural elements.

Tonkin Zulaikha Greer have shown considerable
respect for and understanding of the original
internal architecture. It is therefore ironic that, on
the so-called grounds that they have not been
sufficiently respectful of the original building,
they have been prevented from carrying out the
major task: the provision of a new entry
sequence into the building. This new entry,
which was designed in response to current
circulation problems and future gallery

demands, was to be a six-storey glass-clad
foyer, utilising the most advanced, ecologically
superior, techniques for heating and cooling the
space with water. The dilemma of the project is
ongoing and it is faced with ensuing
controversy. It raises difficult and still unresolved
questions about heritage and moral rights
issues.[H]

Public Space
**The project of the public realm underscores
the work of Tonkin Zulaikha Greer.**

The Rocks Square retail centre demonstrates their
interest in creating new urban settings, and in
wresting public space from private urban
developments wherever possible. Completed in
1993, it earned the Walter Burley Griffin national
urban design award. This project, developed from
a collection of disused but historically important
buildings, is in the Rocks precinct at the base of
the Sydney Harbour Bridge. The building shows
Tonkin Zulaikha Greer's interest in exploring other
architectural sources and testing them in a candid
manner. The new brick and concrete building is,
in its section, strongly informed by the high
vaulted main hall of the ancient Markets of Trajan
in Rome. The building explores the practice's
interest in monumentality and construction
technique, with the work of Louis Kahn providing
an obvious further model. And beyond the
architecture of Rome and Kahn is evidence of the
work of Alison and Peter Smithson with their
concern for a direct use of materials, of detailing
without artifice, of the reality of materials, and
their thickness, weight and surfaces. The process
of construction here informs the aesthetic.

Following on from their earlier public projects,
Tonkin Zulaikha Greer took on the difficult task
of implementing an 'urban glue' that would

visually link the various projects for the 2000 Olympic Games at Homebush Bay in Sydney[6]. They did this primarily through the development of what they describe as a 'suite of systems', an overarching strategy that unites and provides a consistent identity for the sporting venues scattered widely across the Olympic site. The 'suite' (including purpose-designed paving, lighting, signage and street furniture) provides the means of lighting, servicing and definition of the major public spaces.

The most prominent of the elements was a series of nineteen lighting towers or pylons in the Olympic Plaza. Each pylon was named after the nineteen cities that had previously hosted an Olympic Games and was designed to act as a highly visible meeting place, a marker, a direction finder and, in total, as a means of giving scale to the vast open plaza. The pylons are 30 metres high and lean towards the northern sun, away from the main stadium, appearing to stride across the plaza like mechanical monsters in a Star Wars epic. These giant sculptures are ingenious objects with each part performing several functions. The solar collectors powering the lights also offer shade, the towers act as markers and as the means for providing indirect lighting, and the concrete base enables structural stability, enclosures for services, and the named space for meeting. And again there is a formal reference to Constructivism.

With their first project in Melbourne, Tonkin Zulaikha Greer have joined with landscape architects Taylor Cullity Lethlean and artist Robert Owen to design sound control walls and a freeway bridge at Craigieburn, They see this project as another form of the urban realm, one regularly ignored as having potential for architectural intervention. In this instance, the bridge begins as an extended wall in Cor-ten steel, one that waves like a diagonally folded ribbon along the Hume Freeway for two kilometres before leaping across the road at the first sight of the Melbourne CBD, similar to a lifted curtain to the skyline.

Private Space
Tonkin Zulaikha Greer's interest in the public realm has been complemented by their work in the private realm of housing. The practice's work in this area has included developer-led apartment blocks, public housing projects and single houses carefully tailored to individual needs.

It is however, the private house that reinforces the practice's formal diversity. The design methods applied to their residential work are eclectic and respond directly to the processes of building, site and client. Consequently there is no single architectural language or aesthetic that identifies their houses, which range from the architecturally and sculpturally expressive Putney House on Sydney's Parramatta River to the carefully constructed and site-responsive beach houses at Killcare and Pearl Beach. The unifying thread across all of their residential work is their commitment to both environmental and social responsibility.

The house at Lilyfield in Sydney's inner west, designed by Peter Tonkin and Ellen Woolley, convincingly illustrates the practice's interests in dealing with both the public and private aspects of buildings. On the street boundary of a narrow rocky site, a sharp slope at the edge of a busy road, the architects built a three storey wall, derived from the past industrial context of Lilyfield in colour and scale, behind which the slim house is fashioned. Its mottled

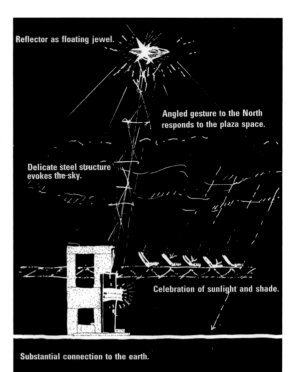

Olympic Plaza Lighting Towers. Architectural concept diagram, 1997.

19

embedded image, formed from the combination of gloss and matt black-glazed bricks, acts like a giant urban painting, both conspicuous and celebratory, changing through the day with the angle of the light.[7][1]

Developer initiated and commercially driven apartment complexes have also played a considerable role in the practice's attitude towards 'private' space. In the past decade there has been a strong population surge in Sydney's inner city and its demographic has been significantly altered. This has brought considerable urban change, which has not only encouraged new development and communities but has also changed the perception of apartment living. The city's reconfigured urban centre has led to the increased development of residential towers and low rise multi unit blocks. These models of living have been traditionally fraught with conflicts in differentiating between public and private space. Tonkin Zulaikha Greer have implemented practical methods that negate these problems and encourage a sense of neighbourhood.

The small apartment block in Challis Avenue, Potts Point, responds to its setting in an imaginative manner. It stitches together the formal qualities of its two neighbours with the use of a protruding orthogonal frame of copper tiles, a whimsical mask grafted onto the body of the building. And two of the six apartments have double volume living spaces, opening out in a celebratory manner to the visual splendour of Sydney. In contrast, the apartment block built in 1995 in Ultimo, designed in association with Roderick Simpson, is a tough and gritty response to the provision of architecture for affordable housing. Although raw and direct, a

real example of a Brutalist building as meant by the Smithsons, it provides dignified housing for the occupants and makes intelligent use of ESD principles. The small apartments relate purposefully to the street, and each makes a direct connection with the public realm.

Tonkin Zulaikha Greer are currently designing two major adaptive re-use apartment projects. One is the planned conversion of grain silos in Newtown, a tough exercise reconciling a disused but iconic industrial building with contemporary residential requirements. Working from the constraining geometry of the concrete cylinders, Tonkin Zulaikha Greer have developed a responsive vocabulary of forms, materials and finishes, maintaining the industrial ethos of the silos.

The other project, now under construction, is the Scots Church redevelopment at Wynyard Park in Sydney's CBD. This project, won through a limited competition, is an ambitious mix that includes the conversion of an existing heritage-listed building and, in its airspace, the design of a new building of residential units. The proposal takes its compositional cues from the neo-Gothic forms of the existing building, supported by the design for the section, which responds to the legislated shadow plane determining the angle of the development. The architects have devised a stepped section using two-level units requiring access only on every second level. The resulting stepped form of the building is silhouetted against the sky as an abstracted echo of the existing building. The design provides wintergardens which offer both acoustic protection and a passive thermal climate filter, structuring the façade in a complementary vertical pattern. The Scots Church redevelopment is an instance of

'Atria'. Street views of the apartment project, for the design competition entry, 2003.

grasping design opportunities offered by the circumstantial.

The Tomb and the Monument

In the early 20th Century, Adolf Loos proposed that 'Only a very small part of architecture belongs to art: the tomb and the monument. Everything else that fulfils a function is to be excluded from the domain of art.'[8] Tombs and monuments, buildings for which the primary aim is not directed to usefulness but to embodying a culture's collective memory, have become almost an area of specialization for Tonkin Zulaikha Greer. They have accepted the challenge set by Loos and wrestled with issues of representation, symbolism and metaphor in a series of such buildings. For Tonkin Zulaikha Greer these buildings offer the opportunity for serious exploration of meaning in their forms. For more than a decade they have been involved with designing significant Australian memorials.

A distinctive aspect of Tonkin Zulaikha Greer's work in this field is the way they work directly with visual artists. In their view, they have learned significantly from the different attitude held by artists to objects, materials, and "physical stuff".[9] They suggest that artists are often more thoughtful than architects about their formal moves and the meaning behind them. As a practice they admire their ability to seize opportunities and challenge conventional responses. Tonkin Zulaikha Greer also have the view that artists often understand scale better than architects. Consequently artists have been invited as collaborators on a number of their competition winning projects. The practice believes that, usually, architects bring visual artists too late in a project's development to embellish an architectural solution. They prefer

I. ELLEN WOOLLEY WAS EMPLOYED BY TONKIN ZULAIKHA GREER IN 1996, AND RESIGNED IN 1998 TO PURSUE AN INDEPENDENT PRACTICE. HER WORK HAS BEEN PRIMARILY OF A DOMESTIC SCALE, WITH SOME PUBLIC PROJECTS DESIGNED IN COLLABORATION WITH ARTISTS.
WOOLLEY AND PETER TONKIN MARRIED IN 2001 AND THEY COLLABORATED ON THEIR OWN HOUSES – AT KILLCARE AND LILYFIELD – BOTH OF WHICH WERE UNDERTAKEN OUTSIDE THE TZG OFFICE.

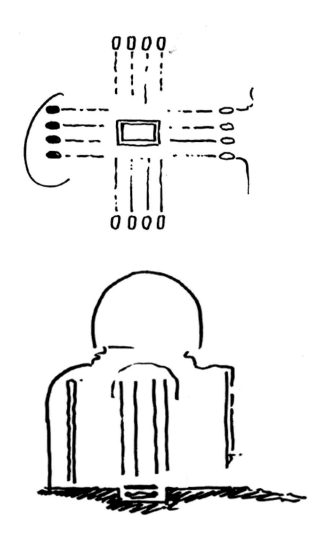

Tomb of the Unknown Australian Soldier. Spatial relationship diagram for competition entry, 1992.

J. KEN UNSWORTH AM, ONE OF AUSTRALIA'S MOST CHALLENGING AVANT-GARDE ARTISTS, BEGAN MAKING SCULPTURE IN 1966 AND HAS BEEN EXHIBITING WORK SINCE THIS TIME. UNSWORTH, WHO ACHIEVED CONSIDERABLE NOTICE IN 1975 WITH THE USE OF HIS OWN BODY IN A SERIES OF PERFORMANCES – '5 SECULAR SETTINGS FOR SCULPTURE AS RITUAL, AND AS BURIAL PLACE', HAS AN EMINENT REPUTATION FOR HIS STRIKING AND MYSTERIOUS INSTALLATION WORK. MUCH OF HIS PRACTICE EXPLORES THE SUBJECT OF THE JOURNEY OF LIFE, EVOKING EMOTIONAL RESPONSE AROUND THE RECOGNITION OF A SENSE OF LOSS OR ABSENCE. IN MANY OF UNSWORTH'S INSTALLATIONS THERE IS A SENSE OF FEAR AND OF SOMBRE TRAGEDY.

MANY OF HIS WORKS EXPLORE THE POWER OF SUSPENDED ELEMENTS, AND THE EARLY DECISION OF THE COLLABORATING DESIGNERS TO UNITE THE THREE 'STELAE' WHICH FORM THE VIETNAM MEMORIAL WITH A RING OR DISC OF SUSPENDED ROCKS PROVED CONTENTIOUS. THEIR EVER-PRESENT SENSE OF DANGER, WHICH WAS A MAJOR ELEMENT IN THE DESIGN, WAS REJECTED BY THE VIETNAM VETERANS, WHO WANTED A MORE SERENE AND REFLECTIVE PLACE. THE STONES WERE ABSTRACTED INTO A CIRCLE OF BLACK GRANITE STONES, UTILIZING THE SAME SUSPENSION SYSTEM, RECALLING A HALO OR THE WHIRRING ROTORS OF A HELICOPTER. ONE OF THE STONES CONTAINS A HIDDEN SCROLL WITH THE NAMES OF THOSE AUSTRALIAN SERVICEMEN WHO DIED IN VIETNAM.

K. JANET LAURENCE IS AN INSTALLATION ARTIST WHOSE WORK HAS BEEN INCLUDED IN MAJOR SURVEY EXHIBITIONS AND COLLECTIONS, NATIONALLY AND INTERNATIONALLY.

JANET LAURENCE'S WORK RESONATES WITH AND ECHOES THE DISCIPLINE OF ARCHITECTURE AND ARCHITECTURAL FORM, WHILE RETAINING ORGANIC QUALITIES AND A SENSE OF TRANSIENCE – AN UNFIXED NESS.

HER PUBLIC COMMISSIONS INCLUDE 'THE EDGE OF THE TREES', AT THE MUSEUM OF SYDNEY; THE AWARD WINNING '49 VEILS' – WINDOWS FOR THE CENTRAL SYNAGOGUE IN SYDNEY; 'THE TOMB OF THE UNKNOWN SOLDIER' IN THE AUSTRALIAN WAR MEMORIAL, CANBERRA WITH TONKIN ZULAIKHA GREER; 'VEIL OF TREES' FOR THE SYDNEY SCULPTURE WALK; 'PICTURE THE DARK FACE OF THE RIVER' COMMISSIONED BY THE DEPARTMENT OF ENVIRONMENT, CANBERRA; 'IN THE SHADOW' AN ENVIRONMENTAL INSTALLATION FOR THE OCA AT OLYMPIC PARK, SYDNEY. SHE MOST RECENTLY COLLABORATED WITH TONKIN ZULAIKHA GREER IN THE DESIGN OF THE AUSTRALIAN WAR MEMORIAL, HYDE PARK, IN LONDON.

to work with artists at the point of gestation of the idea, as equal partners in developing the primary architectural concept.

In 1991, the firm won the competition to design the National Memorial to the Australian Vietnam Forces in Canberra, collaborating with the sculptor Ken Unsworth, who generated a series of ideas seeking a formal resolution of the public interpretation of this controversial war with the more private commemorative needs of the veterans and their families. Tonkin Zulaikha Greer worked with one of the Unsworth ideas, the use of hanging rocks supported in a suspended circle set between inclined and massive blades of concrete, although the rocks were later excluded. The concept offered a gesture of reconciliation between those who opposed the war and those who fought, voluntarily or by conscription. The architects sought to convey a sense of irresolution and conflict held in suspension, a level of abstraction that initially worried the client body and the Vietnam veterans but which met with widespread approval once it was completed.[J]

The Tomb of the Unknown Australian Soldier was another Canberra project won in competition with the collaboration of an artist, this time with Janet Laurence.[K] Set within a buckled floor surface, the Tomb is located in the centre of the Hall of Memory in the Australian War Memorial, a space that has a powerful existing geometry and set of artworks dating from the 1940s.

The mullions of the high memorial windows by Napier Waller [L] **provide the geometric cue for the four pillars by Tonkin Zulaikha Greer and Janet Laurence, which represent in turn the four ancient elements; air, earth, fire, water. They provide the opportunity for the designers to explore their fascination with the nature of materials but also to explore the symbolic potential of these materials.**

The abstraction of the sleek, eleven metre high pillars provides a strong contrast with Waller's figurative imagery in the mosaics and stained glass windows, which represent the defining qualities of Australian servicemen and women. The pillars are placed in an apse, as a visual termination of the major axis that runs from the Hall of Memory, down Anzac Parade, across Lake Burley Griffin and on to Parliament House.

Following this, and after the year 2000 was proclaimed to be the Year of Peace, the Brahma Kumaris Raja Yoga Centres, in a commemorative gesture, funded the construction of a Peace Pavilion. This was a twelve month gift to the city of Sydney and the state of New South Wales. Although originally designed without a fixed site, it came to be located in Centennial Park. The purpose of the pavilion was to provide a place for peaceful contemplation, a place to sit and meditate on the reassuring certainty of the rising sun. The Tonkin Zulaikha Greer design deliberately suspended the possibility of formal resolution. Instead, it embraced impurity as a metaphor for tolerance and suggested that it is only through peace that the disparate elements may be brought together into some fragile form of resolution. The timber floor plane, set at seat height as an extended sitting platform, floated above the grass of the park while the canopy, also a floating timber plane, was curved and battened. The two horizontal leaves of ground and shelter were separated by two heavy piers embellished with selected text on the theme of peace.[M]

The culmination of these projects was the Australian War Memorial at Hyde Park Corner in London, another project won by Tonkin Zulaikha Greer through a limited competition and another collaboration with Janet Laurence. The project had a remarkably short lead time of twelve months from the date the design was selected to its official opening.

Finished for Armistice Day, 2003, the Memorial was built to honour the 1.5 million Australians who fought alongside the British in two World Wars and to commemorate the 101,000 Australian service people who died in these wars. The Memorial wall encloses and protects as it sweeps around the exposed corner, suggestive of an archaic site that has, through geological circumstances, heaved itself back into existence, with exfoliated stone slabs reminiscent of the headstones packed against each other in old disused cemeteries. The stone is a grey-green granite from Jerramungup in Western Australia, a rejection of the initial requirement from English Heritage that the Memorial be built in London's favoured Portland stone. 24,000 place names, as recorded on enlistment papers for the two World Wars, document the birth-places of those who served and died in the Australian Army, Navy and Air Force. Superimposed over, and incorporating the place names, are larger letters, cut more boldly, recording forty-seven battle sites where the Australian and British forces fought together.

The surface of the wall is rich and dense in pattern and suggestion. Text has been an integral design element in all of the memorials by Tonkin Zulaikha Greer.

The London Memorial does not carry the names of the dead but honours the

L. AUSTRALIAN ARTIST M NAPIER WALLER SERVED WITH THE 1ST AIF DURING WORLD WAR I. HE LOST HIS RIGHT ARM AT BULLECOURT IN 1917 AND HAD TO LEARN TO DRAW WITH HIS LEFT HAND. HIS WORK INCLUDES NUMEROUS PUBLIC MURALS AND PAINTINGS, AND IN THE AUSTRALIAN WAR MEMORIAL'S HALL OF MEMORY, ONE OF THE WORLD'S LARGEST MOSAICS COMPRISING MORE THAN SIX MILLION ITALIAN TILES OF 70 DIFFERENT COLOURS, AS WELL AS THE 15 PANELS OF STAINED GLASS IN THREE WINDOWS. BOTH OF THESE WORKS WERE COMPLETED IN THE 1950S, ALTHOUGH DESIGNED EARLIER.

M. THE PEACE PAVILION WAS A TEMPORARY SYDNEY INSTALLATION FOR THE INTERNATIONAL YEAR OF PEACE IN 2000. IT HAS BEEN REMOVED FROM CENTENNIAL PARK AND RE-ERECTED IN COFFS HARBOUR IN NORTHERN NSW.

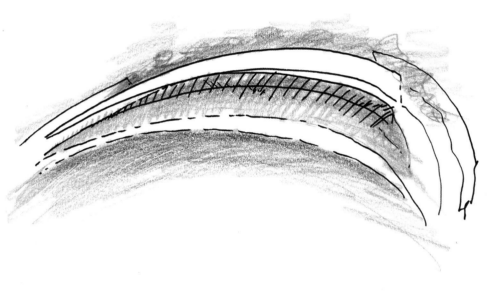

Australian War Memorial, London. Concept sketch drawn on site, 2002.

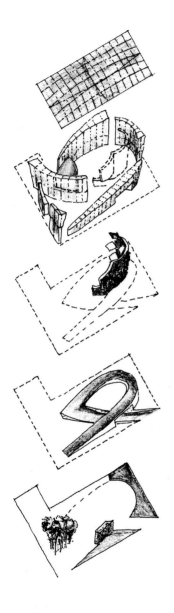

communities that bred, supported and grieved for these service people. The Hyde Park Memorial can be compared to Maya Ying Lin's Vietnam Veteran's Memorial in Washington DC, as it invites speculation and reflection. However, unlike the Washington memorial, it has been built so long after the events commemorated that it subverts the nationalist sentiment normally evoked in war memorials, carefully avoiding the didactic. Instead, it becomes a dignified meditation on the 20th Century history of Australia.

Tonkin Zulaikha Greer's work embraces the qualities of Sydney. It responds positively and knowledgeably to its built fabric, and is directed to improving its urbanity. The architects work in the city, extracting maximum possible architectural opportunities from limited budgets and apparently everyday commissions. They relate purposefully to existing buildings, recuperating and then enhancing them with their additions and, in the process, converting the prosaic into the poetic. Operating in a corporate world they are able to develop non-corporate solutions, tailored and made particular for each job. As a measure of their ability they have won an unusually high number of the awards and competitions in which they've entered. In accepting the process of urban development as accretion over time, Tonkin Zulaikha Greer have a clear understanding of their own contribution to the ongoing project of Sydney, and, by extension, of all cities.

Footnotes

1   TZG in conversation with the author, 8 August and 1 November 2003.
2   R. Banham, The New Brutalism: Ethic or Aesthetic?, London: The Architectural Press, 1966, p.85.
3   J. Baker, 'A Smithson File', Arena, February 1966, pp.177 217 (p.183). See also, G. London, 'The Canon of New Brutalism – an alternative reading through the work of Alison and Peter Smithson', in Conference Proceedings from Society of Architectural Historians of Australia and New Zealand, Melbourne 1998, pp.189–196.
4   The term, 'Brutalist', has been applied most recently by Naomi Stead in 'A Little Brutalist Castle', Architecture Australia, July/August 2003, pp.68–75, a discussion of TZG's Lilyfield house.
5   The Historic Houses Trust of New South Wales.
6   Tonkin Zulaikha Greer worked with Hargreaves Landscape Architects and Masterplanners, and led a team comprising, Hassell (paving), Emery Vincent Design (graphics) Barry Webb and Associates (lighting design) and KWA (industrial design).
7   For a full discussion on the Tonkin/Woolley house see Naomi Stead, 'A Little Brutalist Castle', Architecture Australia, July/August 2003, pp.68–75.
8   Adolf Loos, 'Architecture', 1910, reprinted in The Architecture of Adolf Loos, The Arts Council of Great Britain, London, 1985, p.108.
9   TZG in conversation with the author, 8 August and 1 November 2003.

Australian Pavilion at Hannover. Components drawing for competition entry, 1998.

'Bones'. The structure of the 'Portico' apartment tower as it rises from the 1920s Scots Church base.

Architecture and 'The Other'
A Manifesto

Architecture dwells in 'the other' – it is created and has its existence in the spaces beyond and between those of mere pragmatism. Without denying the primary importance to the users, and to us as designers, of a well-built functional object, this is, however, nothing more than the means to the architect's desired end: a work of architecture. Here, the carefully-nurtured 'other' is manifest, creating an awareness of the life beyond a simple physical existence. The enduring presence and significance of this architectural creation speaks to the mind and the spirit. This may be called the art of architecture; without it we are merely building.

In making this other, the additions to the functional program of a building are often beyond what is briefed, occasionally they must be slid past an uncaring client. To preserve the professionalism and ethical position of the architect, such architectural concerns must have no negative impact on the brief requirements or on the wider social issues of building: not increasing the budget or reducing the functionality of the work. Further, they must not be patronisingly intellectual or beyond the comprehension of the users, they must relate to the building's place and time.

For TZG, the art of architecture, this sense of the 'other', is achieved through meaning and metaphor, sculpture and light; through controlled sequences of spaces, the sparing use of iconography, the recalling of memory and the embodiment of ideas. The practice's buildings, wide in range, divergent in aims, are developed in many ways; each related to the site, the brief, the city, the users and (of course) the current obsessions of the designers.

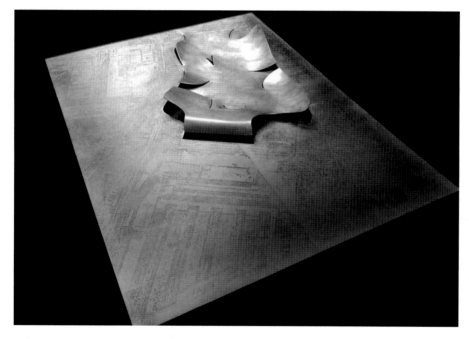

Belmore Park collaborative design project by Robyn Backen, Danny Venlet and Peter Tonkin for 'Making The City', Artspace, 1992.

Architecture and the City

Whilst most of the work of the practice has been in the greater Sydney area, the qualities of this place have informed work undertaken elsewhere.

Sydney's *zeitgeist* seems to require architecture of strength and weight. Its wondrous rich landscape overpowers the delicate work that sits so well in the tropical north, and resists the emphasis on form and surface that pervades Melbourne architecture. Here the light and the landform need sculptural forms and unfinished materials. Recent Sydney architecture adopts either an early Modernist denial of materiality in favour of pure form and colour, as exemplified by many recent Minimalists, or recalls European high-tech or neo-Brutalist work, a continuation of the 'Sydney School' of the 1960s and 70s– a softer and more naturalistic Brutalism. A third identifiable Sydney school is the architectural shed or light open pavilion, often a sophisticated Miesian development of the simple vernacular form. In much of this recent Sydney work, the concerns of material fall between Melbourne's abstraction and Brisbane's expressiveness, and the informing ideas are purely architectural rather than semiotic or tectonic. TZG has resisted Minimalism, in favour of the tectonic celebration of the built artefact – 'maximilism'? – in a contemporary urbanised translation of the arcadian 'Sydney School'. Another aspect to the city – its brassy commercialism – makes Sydney the country's 'great whore'. This opportunism can allow the architect a level of experiment with the creation of constructed 'special effects' which may be ephemeral, as well as suggesting a degree of playful image-making in the public realm.

Material and Form

The practice's continued obsession with the universality of meaning in architectural language manifests in developed hierarchies of material and form. Whether consciously or not, an architect determines the materials of a potential building almost as soon as it is conceived – so innate is the materiality to the architecture. Materials are the vehicle of architecture – the way it is made physically extent and enduring, comprehensible and useable. Architecture is created at the union of built function and built idea, and material is the manifestation of both of these intentions.

TZG has always preferred buildings to be made of materials which are unfinished and direct. Natural materials such as stone and timber, now becoming luxuries, are strategically related to areas of high occupancy. Brick and concrete are used as a thick or solid matrix which holds the building together. Steel, with its demanding grammar of connection and exciting delicacy, is celebrated for its sculptural richness. Thin cladding is used only where necessary, preferably in unfinished durable metal – copper, stainless steel, zinc. The articulation of these materials, in contrast to the formless whiteness of the early Moderns, produces the depth and delight of the building.

Set against and interweaving with the 'positive' of the building's material – floor, walls and roof – is the 'negative' of the spaces which this physicality produces, inside and out. It is this interweaving and balancing of solid and void, space and material that becomes the reality of architecture.

To direct and organise the spaces and forms of a building, formal gesture is used in many of TZG's projects as a basis for design. Whilst founded on an understanding of social and architectural history, this is in no sense historicist, rather using the continuum of our culture to place gestures related to the concerns of the present. The risk of formalism is avoided by a pragmatic approach to planning and function, and a delight in complexity.

Space and Movememt

If material is the physical presence of architecture, then its spaces are its life. In a time when the Modernist *espace libre* has become ubiquitous, the modulation and articulation of space becomes a necessity, creating controlled and ordered sequences of movement and occupation, where the life of a building is nurtured. The physical progression through space requires a movement between

Surfrider pavilion for Darling Harbour. Model, 1999.

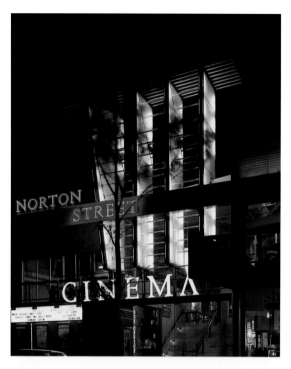

states of memory and anticipation, the evolving comprehension of an environment.

Spaces are linked both by paths and by sight: views from one space to another become key linkages in the continuum of the work, the whole is revealed by a series of views and long vistas. The openings that reveal these connections are developed as layered devices of joining and separation, places where construction and function are elaborated.

The act of moving through the building – across and especially up and down – is celebrated to produce a defining experience of light and architecture. Stairs and escalators, lifts and ramps, these are the elements of dynamism, related to the experience of the vertical and the changing quality of space. In our work they are central architectural elements, never hidden, never fully enclosed. In small buildings the stair becomes a major focus, in large works systems of vertical transport are the heart of the architecture.

Activity and Light

Spaces without occupation become meaningless. The uses of space in TZG's buildings are carefully controlled so that major parts of the public realm are enlivened by activity, and this activity is drawn through space into the fabric of the work. In commercial and cultural buildings there is a progression from open busy spaces at the core of the building outwards to more enclosed private 'rooms'. In houses, the living spaces relate to the circulation, the sequence of entry and the external environment. Living becomes both a theatre of movement and a stage of repose.

To demarcate the places of activity, light is a continuing obsession. Daylight, controlled by screens and other built elements, becomes both functional and dynamic, a crucial element in the occupation of an interior. Artificial light supplements natural light and dramatises the architecture, highlighting selected surfaces and forms, whilst providing task-specific requirements. A continuous ambience is avoided.

Externally, both day and night lighting bring the forms and surfaces of a building into life. This *chiaroscuro*, changing with location, climate and aspect, has always been a fundamental part of architecture. Its interaction with comfort and with the drama of architectural form makes daylight a major determinant in design. Night image, especially in relation to the paces of the city, gives the designer a chance to work an alchemic transformation, dissolving the material and altering the three-dimensional perception of forms. In many projects TZG have created, with careful management, night-time landmarks where light and surface become one.

Durability and Conscience

Increasingly, architects have become the conscience of the building industry, adopting sustainable design principles in advance of and beyond legal requirements. TZG has embraced ESD as a philosophy to be integrally celebrated in the architecture, not to be hidden or added on. In many instances, the whole expression of the work is based on the sustainable system adopted, the required forms and technology being fundamental to the way the building is shaped and detailed.

A major and often overlooked component of ESD is the life-time durability of the building.

top
Norton Street Cinemas,
1997.

above
Avalon house,
computer model,
2004.

28

Much of the energy consumed by buildings is lost in repeated refitting, repair and alteration – or in premature demolition. A durable artefact will be usable long into the future, the embodied energy of its initial construction being 'amortised' over many years, the economy of its sound energy performance providing continual benefits to many users and owners. More active environmental systems tend to be both more experimental and more initially costly. They must be used with care and in well-considered combination with more durable passive design principles.

Practice and Pragmatics

TZG is a practice which has developed a very high level of collaboration between its staff members. A single team will take each project through from inception to completion. Each project, the responsibility of one or more of the directors, is 'owned' by those who work on it, there is no separate design and production office, and expertise at construction is shared across the range of projects.

This enables details to be developed at pre- and post-construction stages to reinforce the initial design ideals. It also enables the inevitable changes to the design resulting from client and authority input – and from the accidents of on-site construction – to be integrated into the design, strengthening it rather than undermining it, reinforcing the design intent of the entire project.

The approach and methods of the practice allow the generative potential of each project to evolve by responding to the specifics of the place, the client and the creators. This developing life force becomes the informing basis of each design, ensuring that each retains its individuality, each responds in its unique way. There is no consistent, limiting 'house style': work has great depth, achieving a wide diversity of detail and approach. The project team commit to working single-mindedly to achieve in the completed work the power of the sketch

In many projects, TZG have worked with selected artists from the initial concept stage, so that there is no division between the art and the architecture. The formal and metaphysical concerns of the artist are integrated with the architecture, each informing and enriching the other. Built work such as memorials and galleries are based on a high level of collaboration, and the successful public project is highly rewarding. Theoretical projects, installations and gallery work are further from the constraints of function and durability, allowing more polemic explorations of form and content.

Scale and Appropriateness

Consistently, a sense of the broader responsibility of the architect has underpinned the work of the practice. This has two aspects – one relates to the consideration of the building's context and the other to the design of the building itself. With both, scale is a decisive element, relating the size of spaces and built forms to the individual and to the context.

A consideration of the surroundings does not imply a purely contextualist basis for architecture – rather a symbiotic relationship of place and building; with the making of a landmark an appropriate action in the correct circumstance. However, for many projects there is no appropriate genesis for the extraordinary, and thus buildings are part of a greater whole, suiting either the importance of a historic neighbourhood or the anonymous program of the building itself. Context also defines the fixed parameters of a site – aspect, sunlight, privacy and air movement, which control the fundamental design of a building.

This sense of appropriateness also pervades the approach to the design of the building as an object. It is sensible to put effort, equalling cost in either design time or construction, where it will be of most benefit. It is unrealistic to expect elaborate monumentality from a simple commercial building, and the client must be in sympathy with the architectural intentions of any house. Conversely, a major public building or monument demands an architecture responsive to the highest aspirations of the society which commissions it. The old expression – "you must cut your coat to suit your cloth" – sums up a pragmatic approach which ensures that effort is rewarded.

The Power of Creation

Architects have a unique ability to experiment with one-off creations which are actually used in everyday life. This power to build, to create real objects, underlies the fascination of the work, and exposes its danger: to avoid self-indulgence on one side and subservience on the other. This however is the path the designer must follow. Tonkin Zulaikha Greer's work is ongoing, developing its exploration of the possibilities of architectural practice, building on the pragmatic to create realised manifestations of a powerful 'other'.

following page
National Memorial to
the Australian Vietnam
Forces Canberra,
1990-1992. Detail.

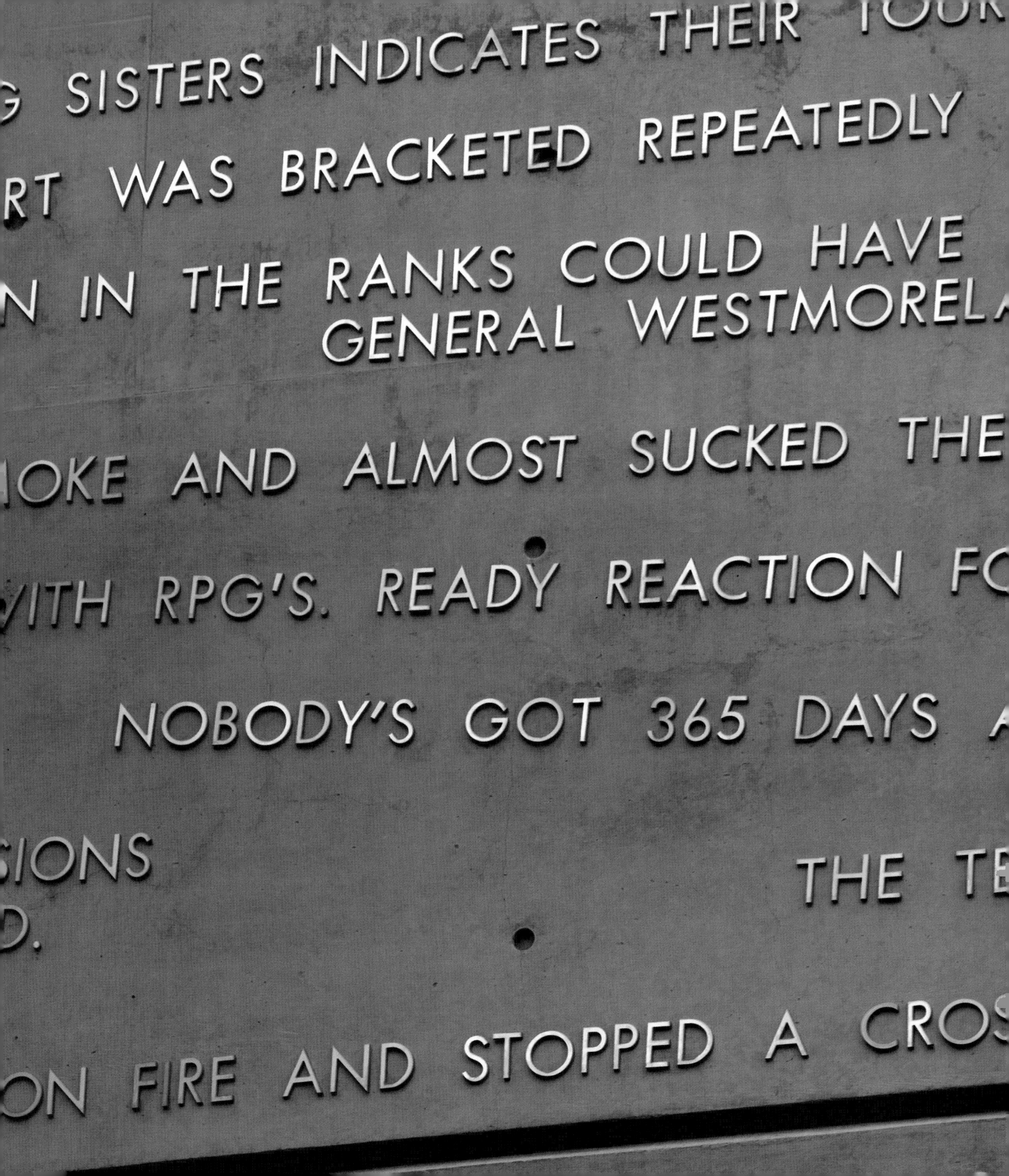

G SISTERS INDICATES THEIR TOUR

RT WAS BRACKETED REPEATEDLY

N IN THE RANKS COULD HAVE
GENERAL WESTMOREL A

IOKE AND ALMOST SUCKED THE

VITH RPG'S. READY REACTION FO

NOBODY'S GOT 365 DAYS A

SIONS
D.

THE TE

ON FIRE AND STOPPED A CROS

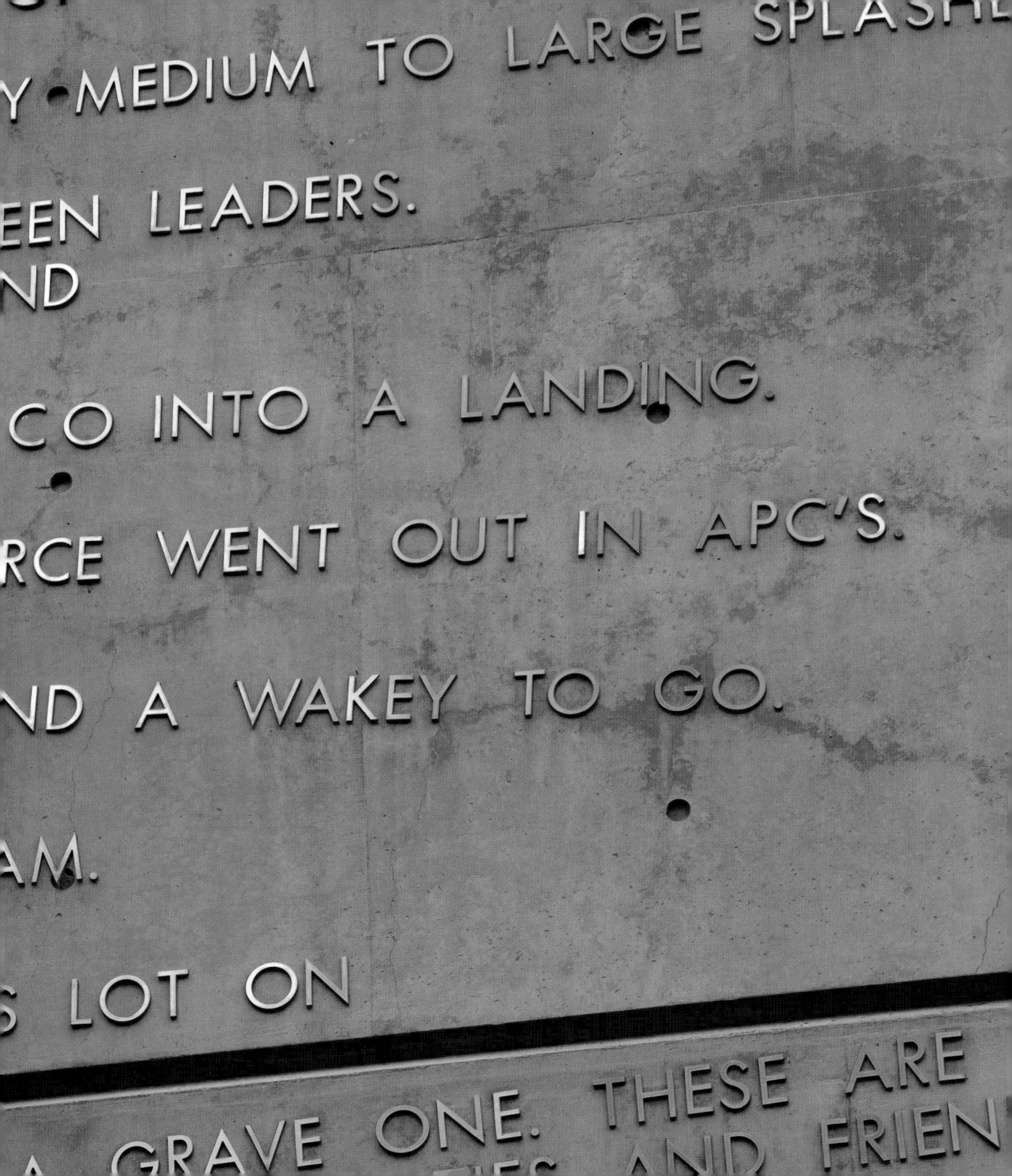

...MEDIUM TO LARGE SPLASH...

...EEN LEADERS.

...ND

...CO INTO A LANDING.

...RCE WENT OUT IN APC'S.

...ND A WAKEY TO GO.

...AM.

...S LOT ON

...A GRAVE ONE. THESE ARE

...ES AND FRIEND...

Peter Emmett

The TZG office
atmosphere and urbanity

It's strange that they call it 'the office', this studio workplace. It just doesn't seem like an office. From the Surry Hills rag-trade days, a bold deco(-ish) façade muscles its presence between the quiet Metropolitan Electroplaters and the loud Numero Uno cafe. Enter a contemporary reception area, the friendly space an eerie contrast with a wall of Rosemary Laing's 'Brownwork #9', a giant photograph inside the belly of a cargo plane. Beyond is the conference room where collaborations and contracts are created and contested. The space is bathed in light and the lyrical gestures of Brian Blanchflower's 'Orcadian Light'. Next is a transitional space, a suite of small rooms strewn with models, magazines, the office library, more artworks, the TZG directors and many notes and sketches for colleagues. Here is where Peter, Brian and Tim share space and imaginaries.

From here the office explodes into a dramatic zone that is part factory, studio and performance space. There are many desks with big computers, and chunks of stone and steel, models, prototypes and specimens. It's like a museum of ambiguous objects. There is also a kitchen with many usable things, and wonderful smells of use. An outdoor area has a gigantic table that would seat all staff and guests with gusto. And it frequently does. A handwritten sign warns that it's obligatory to have communal teas in this office, and there are embarrassing penalties for non-compliance. Such is the desire for the sharing of private and public pleasures at TZG.

The office is flooded with raw outside light and frequently with raucous inside laughter. This place has atmosphere! Baudrillard, that

architect of imaginary word worlds, describes the qualities of 'atmosphere' as play, calculation, substance and abstraction. This is a fine description of the TZG workspace. People working with proverbial blood, sweat and tears, and with practical phone, computer and paper. More often it's with each other, consulting, critiquing, collaborating. There is a quality of calm, even casualness in this atmosphere. This is the space for creative energy and flow. Experience, trust, friendship, knowledge and know-how. These are personal qualities but they translate into professional practice, and into projects.

And what remarkable projects. Today Julie negotiates a sea of iron columns to accommodate a contemporary performance artspace in the Eveleigh railway carriageworks. Kon and Bettina adjust the geometry of apartments inside Newtown concrete silos. Paul and Wolfgang fine-tune construction details for more apartments towering above a

Sydney city church. John models another CBD apartment complex, tracing a fine line between private development managers and the public domain. Liz steps apartments down a hillside in Queenstown snow country while Ruth positions new houses on Manly harbour headlands. Trina is working on new theatres and galleries next to a crowded Port Macquarie shopping mall while Roger and Julie tease them into the cavernous Casula Powerhouse. Neil, Heidi and Kon traverse 18 kilometres of soundwalls along the Craigieburn freeway while Heidi is absorbed in a meticulous adaptation of the monumental marble Reserve Bank. This extraordinary mix of projects, people, programs, sites and spaces, concepts, craft and materials is an ordinary day at the office. The atmosphere of this office, like architecture, is in the mix.

Is it possible that the spirit of the people who conceive imaginary spaces is infused into them, into their atmosphere, substance and

being? Office into architecture? What becomes of the warmth exuded by the TZG office for instance? It's not that cheery sort of warmth, but a rich, resonant and enduring warmth. Like wood has warmth. Wood draws its substance from the earth, it lives and breathes and labours. It has latent warmth because it burns from within. It has *being*. Where does such passion go? Sometimes heat wants quenching with an atmosphere of cool. Like glass is cool, with innate qualities of abstraction. Glass is both material used and ideal imagined: transparency and transcendence. Wood and glass, warm and cool, passion and abstraction, atmosphere and architecture.

Memorable and enduring places, whether apartments, artspaces, theatres, towers, homes or cities, are created through intimate encounter with site and story, material and memory, others and otherness, as well as steel and glass and wood. This is the materiality of the imagination, the substance of dreams, the breathing present. This is more than city building, or urban design: it's urbanity, a palpable feeling of urban pleasures.

Urban pleasures are very serious for the practice of architects like TZG. A mindfulness about the touch of stone on skin as much as its look, or texture or structural substance; the glare of glass on eyes as much as cool reflections in photographs, the warmth of wood and weathering. An architecture of stains, shadows and moods as much as material substance. These too are the qualities of 'atmosphere' that pervade the TZG office and transfer into their architecture. One informs the other, flows into the other, an architecture of atmosphere and urbanity.

Contents

Tonkin Zulaikha Greer Projects

LAW COURTS
& OFFICES
1887-1979

IMMIGRATION
DEPOT
1848-1886

CONVICT
BARRACKS
1819-1848

Francis Greenway's 1817 Hyde Park Barracks is one of Australia's most significant buildings, and has been reinvented, following detailed restoration and refitting, as a new museum "of itself".

Adopting the strictest approach to the conservation and interpretation of its complex layers of heritage fabric, the project was painstakingly developed with the client and heritage authorities, with comprehensive advice from conservation architects Clive Lucas Stapleton and Partners. A continuing process of site investigation, research and briefing covered every aspect of the project, formalising an approach to the fabric and the required new fittings, services and display 'hardware'. The philosophy of each detail was discussed from concept to finished drawing, with the aim of both conserving and communicating the various phases of occupation of the 175-year old Barracks.

The design responds to the differing functions and the degree of 'intactness' of the three levels of the building. The ground floor, which was least intact, has the highest level of new intervention. A focus space at the entry uses the layered removal of later fabric to dramatically illustrate the impact of the successive occupants of the building.

The Greenway Gallery is a special exhibition space of 250 square metres with full conservation-standard air conditioning and lighting, and a flexible system of display panels and showcases, which were purpose designed for the Barracks. The second level reflects the Victorian-period occupancy, and accommodates displays including an Archaeology Room, where a new floating construction of steel and glass contains many of the artefacts found on the site. **The third level was reconstructed to its Greenway-era state.**

One room contains hammocks with timber support framing, to show the sleeping conditions of the convicts, while other spaces are left relatively empty to let the ghosts of the past speak. The three levels of the building are linked by a delicate steel sculpture that recreates the handrail of a vanished stairway.

Original surfaces were conserved with the surviving finish intact, while non-original surfaces were either repainted in colours determined from scrapes, or left a neutral colour. All new work is clearly distinguishable, and has a deliberately strong architectural character to bring the present and the past together, giving each its own clear identity.

Left
The Artefact Case on the ground floor, with a chronological sequence of objects associated with the Barracks.

Right
The western façade of the main Barracks building, designed by Francis Greenway.

Hyde Park Barracks Museum

1989-1991

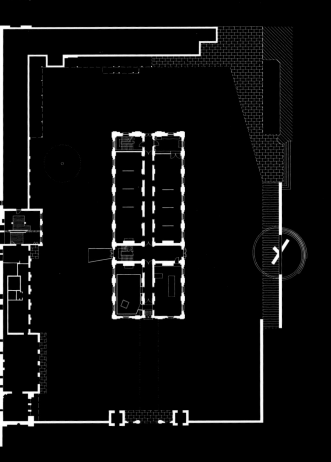

below
The 'Ghost Stair' traces the handrail of the original southern stair, removed in the 19th Century.

right
Reconstructed convict hammocks on the third level of the building.

right
The 'Farnsworth House'
showcase on the second level,
used for changing exhibitions.

below
Installation by Heather
Dorrough on the
reconstructed third level.

opposite
Greenway's original
limewashed roof structure,
formerly concealed by a 19th
Century ceiling.

Royal Blind Society of NSW Library Services Building

Enfield
1990–1991

This programmatically complex building was constructed under the constraints of a very limited budget for a specialised client. It is a major insertion into the existing facilities of the Blind Society and was designed to link and complement its original buildings. The new building includes broadcast-quality sound studios and an audio tape production unit, a reference library, and lending and production facilities for both talking and braille books.

The Library required detailed briefing and specialised design to take account of the needs of sight-impaired and blind workers and visitors. Signage, colours, textured finishes and natural and artificial lighting, as well as more conventional accessibility considerations, were developed to orientate users and distinguish the various spaces.

The sound studios are lined in a mix of timber and hard and soft surfaces to enable the reverberation to be tuned for specific needs, and to create a high-quality environment for the performers. A central day-lit double storey spine provides orientation and address for all of the major facilities, and links the existing buildings on each side of the new Library.

above left
The daylit gallery provides access and orientation within the building.

left
The recording studios.

opposite
The western façade of the building rises above the 1970s concrete boundary walls.

right
An exhibition gallery within
the former Boiler House, with
retained coal hoppers and
access ways.

opposite
The new glass canopy at the
northern entrance.

Powerhouse Regional Arts Centre

Casula
1992–2004

The Casula Powerhouse is a heritage-listed former power station on the banks of the Georges River, 25km south west of the centre of Sydney. It is located in a rapidly growing, ethnically diverse area. Strong community support confirmed the need for a multi-use cultural centre, and an extensive and detailed process of consultation was undertaken for the briefing and design of the Powerhouse, creating a large Regional Gallery with arts production and performance spaces. The Powerhouse serves a range of professional and community groups in the region as well as accommodating touring productions, special exhibitions and major one-off events. The comprehensive facilities are robust and simply operated, ensuring affordable use by the economically constrained local community.

The heritage building has been conserved, with minimal removal of the original fabric, including the remaining coal hoppers and steel access system. New facilities have been carefully fitted into the dramatic, large scale spaces. The major volume – the Turbine Hall – is a multi-use space for large scale activities including parties, exhibitions and performances. A number of specialised studios, galleries, and support areas are fitted into the smaller volumes of other parts of the building. Original interior and exterior surfaces were left unpainted, retaining the patina of use from its life as a power station. New materials are simple and inexpensive, responding to the need for maximum durability and economy. Services are exposed and relate to the preservation of the original wiring and lighting.

The first two stages incorporated gallery, studio, office and rehearsal spaces, and the shell of a future theatre. These were opened in October 1994, and include the conservation of the 30m smoke stack. A range of commissioned public artworks includes 'Christ Knows, a reworking of the major western façade windows by Robyn Backen, the Koori Floor Piece by Judy Watson and local tribes, 'Roll Call' by Nicole Ellis and 'From Outhouse to Arthouse' a community ceramic frieze in the new toilets. External landform sculpting is by Anton James.

The third stage of work, currently under construction, includes the fitout of the 250 seat theatre, a new climate-controlled temporary exhibition gallery, a restaurant, a bookshop and office spaces. Future stages will provide studio space in the upper levels of the building and community art facilities in the old water tanks.

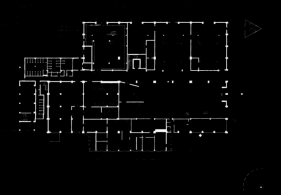

opposite
The original Turbine Hall
houses a large-scale
exhibition and performance
space, with a floor piece by
Judy Watson.

above
Ground floor plan.

above right
New and existing galleries line
the Turbine Hall.

right
Robyn Backen's 'Christ
Knows' in the windows of the
original Boiler House.

below
View from the entry ramp into
the interior.

below right
One of a group of concept
sketches by Ken Unsworth for
the Memorial, 1990.

National Memorial to the Australian Vietnam Forces

Canberra
1990–1992

Designed in collaboration with leading Australian sculptor Ken Unsworth AM, the National Memorial to the Australian Vietnam Forces on Anzac Parade, was completed in October 1992, following an Australia-wide competition.

Dedicated to "all those who served, suffered and died", the Vietnam Memorial resolves the occasionally conflicting needs of public interpretation of this contentious war on the one hand, and the more private commemoration of the war veterans on the other.

The memorial incorporates text, representational art work and sculpture in an organic unified whole. A surrounding moat of water defines the solemn contemplative centre; this domed 'island', linked to Anzac Parade by a broad ramp, is the focus of the rotated triangular composition.

The ring of granite stones suspended between the three 9m high concrete 'stelae' contains a roll of names of those killed in the war, and symbolises the journey from earth to heaven. The focus of the memorial is a 1967 photograph of Australian servicemen at Phouc Tuy in Vietnam, sandblasted into 200 triangular polished granite slabs, each a different size. A second stele wall shows a selection of contemporary quotations, spelled out in stainless steel letters set into the concrete. The third wall, behind the focal monolithic granite 'altar', is blank.

Constructed of high-quality off-form concrete, black granite and stainless steel, the project required sophisticated 3D modelling for the detailing of its complex curved surfaces.

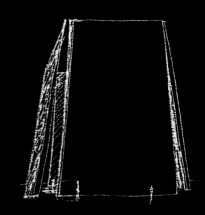

The Tomb of the Unknown Australian Soldier

Canberra
1992–1993

The Tomb of the Unknown Australian Soldier, at the symbolic centre of the Hall of Memory in the Australian War Memorial, was designed in collaboration with artist Janet Laurence. The design is the focus of the War Memorial and was won through a limited competition. It addresses the relationship between war and society and the contemporary relevance of the commemoration of war. It represents a major commitment by the War Memorial to continuing the nation's recognition of its service men and women.

The design responds to the symbolically powerful Napier Waller mosaics and figurative windows that line the domed Hall. The Tomb itself takes the form of an excavated tumulus, in red Rosso Daniel marble. The gilded inscription was hand-drawn and carved.

Four 11 metre tall free-standing pillars are placed in the adjoining niche, each symmetrical with the mosaic-clad mullions of the three major stained glass windows. These pillars represent, in material form, the four Platonic elements – glass for water, stone for earth, nickel silver for fire and jarrah timber for air. Their pure abstract presence enriches the representational complexity of the mosaic and stained glass, and the careful selection of materials, including pure white hand-cast glass, confirms the dominant red-gold colour of the original mosaics.

On 11 November 1993, the 75th anniversary of the Armistice, the Tomb was the focus of a full state funeral of the Unknown Soldier, exhumed from a World War 1 grave at Villiers Bretonneux in France.

right and below
Plan and section of the Tomb within the Hall of Memory.

far right
The Tomb in the centre of the Hall, with the glass, stone, metal and timber pillars in the mosaic-lined niche.

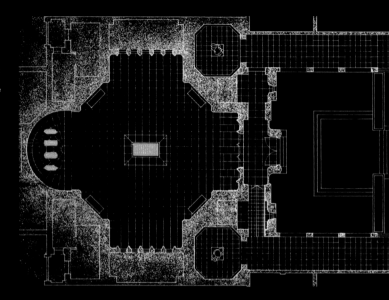

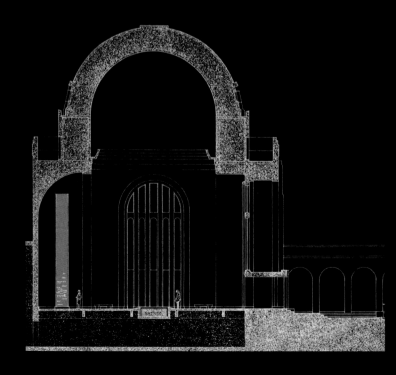

Birchgrove House

1994

Built on a very limited budget, this project added a second floor to a small 1920s single storey fibre-cement cottage to take advantage of harbour views. The house is located between much larger Victorian houses in a gentrified harbour-side suburb.

The design retains the surfaces and details of the original house, and adds a simple new layer of timber and metal to differentiate the new from the old. Detailing is direct and deliberately raw. The arc of the roof, supported by curved steel beams, encloses a timber-lined open plan living space. Bedrooms and work areas are located on both levels.

left and above
A simple curved roof in steel
and timber unites the various
spaces in the upper level.

below
South elevation of the house,
showing the original lower
level and the new upper
storey.

ohn and Drew's Kitchen

irchgrove
000

 new pavilion containing a glass kitchen was
dded to the back of a grand, handsome but neg-
ected Victorian House in the inner west of Sydney.
   It is conceived as a linear room addressing the
arden. The scenario is a wonderful long dining
able set formally on the grass – the guests usu-
lly including at least one celebrity chef (Tony
ilson and Tetsuya Wakuda were consulted on
he equipment) and the show on offer being the
heatre of preparation of the meal.
   The room is a simple glazed element. The details
re careful, meeting without matching the existing
ouse. A strict requirement was to preserve a
umber of plants along the kitchen's garden wall,
equiring the glazing to subtly shift to miss the roots.

right
The new kitchen wing extends
as a glass pavilion in the

The Rocks Square unites three underused buildings as a two level boutique retail centre focused on a new urban square, below four residential apartments. It is located in the heart of The Rocks – Sydney's leading tourist and heritage precinct, and accommodates 60 specialist retail shops and cafes.

The conservation and refurbishment of the 1918 Penrhyn House, and the reconstruction of the adjoining 1970s car park into a mixed-use facility created a civic focus for The Rocks. New façades, deeply modelled and carefully-articulated, envelop the 1970s building, and relate to adjoining large-scale Colonial and Victorian warehouses. Both levels have multiple entrances from the surrounding streets and lanes. A new glass-roofed portico provides a major covered public gallery facing onto the Square.

Detailed urban design analysis of the surrounding environment was required to ensure the new work complemented Sydney's 'Historic Village'. These investigations influenced the design of new colonnades and the square itself, as well as the upgrading of the surrounding streets.

Materials were selected to match the stone, brick and render of the neighbouring Victorian residential and warehouse buildings, and have been left unfinished where possible. Face brick matches the colour of the convict-made sandstock bricks, and sandstone is used as paving and for walls to the public spaces. The interior is defined with expressive hardwood detailing and purpose-designed light fittings.

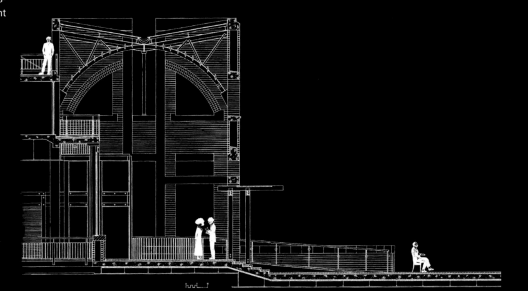

left
Interior of the portico.

above right
The urban scale of the new
main façade defines the
sandstone-paved square.

right
Section of the portico
showing the original building
to the rear.

Affordable Housing Project

Ultimo
1994–1995

A five storey group of 33 low-cost public housing apartments, designed in association with Sydney architect Rod Simpson, and undertaken by a government development corporation (City West) to provide subsidised housing in one of Sydney's most densely built-up areas. The project pioneered the use of environmentally sustainable principles for a medium-rise residential project in an urban environment.

The project was constructed from a limited budget and designed as two parallel blocks, separated by a private communal courtyard which takes advantage of the northern sun. The taller southern block is built to the street edge, and mediates between the differing scales of the adjoining heritage-listed buildings. All apartments run through the building blocks from front to back to maximise sunlight and ventilation. On the northern side of each block, the apartments have lobbies with sliding translucent screens, which double as internal circulation and indoor-outdoor private living space. The southern façades are more restrained, and are built using thermally dense masonry in a self-finished render.

The client-initiated brief was for public housing with 'robust and ecologically superior' design solutions, and the design team utilized materials with low toxicity, low energy-use and minimal processing. These materials, in combination with passive solar design, solar heating and water recycling, created a significant early 'green' project.

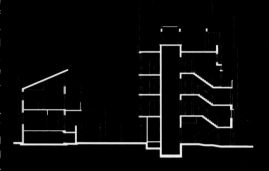

left
The south façade to Macarthur Street.

above right
Section.

right
Private north-facing balconies have sliding screens for weather protection.

Verona Cinemas

Paddington
1994–1996

A four-screen cinema complex with restaurant, office and retail components, the Verona utilises a disused two storey brick and concrete industrial building on Oxford Street, Paddington. Verona has been the catalyst to the resurgence of a previously inactive part of a well-known commercial street.

A new cinema complex of 730 seats was placed on the roof of the building, with retail and other functions below. The auditoria are articulated as a series of metal-clad boxes, with an attached glass foyer overlooking the city and the Harbour. A promenade staircase was developed as a sculptural link to the various levels, lit by an elevated glass roof lantern, which marks the street corner.

Internally, the original concrete structure of the building is left exposed, a contrast to the selection of metals – zinc, aluminium, stainless steel – and the white glass and grey stone used for the circulation zone. The upper-level foyer and the cinemas are enriched with traditional vibrant reds.

opposite
The Oxford Street corner is crowned by a glass lantern and plant tower.

above right
The cinema entry.

right
The third-level cinema foyer with its daylight lantern and views to Sydney Harbour.

elow
hird level plan.

ottom
erona Street elevation.

ght
he main stair, with an
uminium clad balustrade
nd soffit, threads through the
iginal concrete structure.

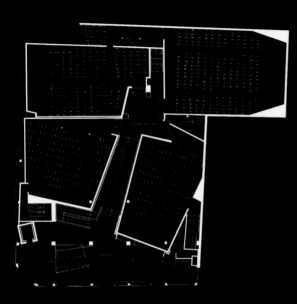

Large sliding screens separate the formal living, kitchen and dining rooms.

Bayview House

1994–1996

Located on a generous waterfront site in a northern suburb of Sydney, this house required flexible planning for occupancy by a couple or by a large extended family.

The 650 square metre house has five bedrooms and extensive formal and informal living spaces. All rooms take full advantage of the established landscaped gardens and northerly views of Pittwater. The house is arranged as a sequence of three parallel gabled pavilions, with linking flat roofed galleries. The pantiled roofs are raised above the thickened masonry walls, allowing natural light and ventilation, while the thick walls accommodate sliding screens and storage.

The house relies on passive environmental control in both summer and winter, and has minimum reliance on mechanical systems. Natural materials appropriate to the site's context have been used in the construction of the house, including timber floors, brick and sandstone walls, and terracotta roofing. The footprint of the house was carefully resolved to conserve the mature garden, notably an established grapevine that was retrained onto the new redwood pergola.

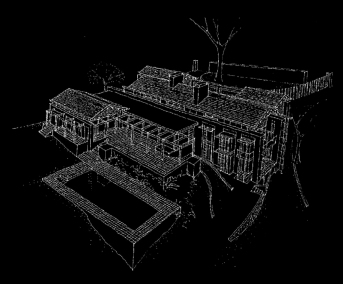

left
Redwood pergolas shade the northern façade.

below left
The terrace with a 50 year-old grapevine.

below
Ground floor plan.

bottom
Section.

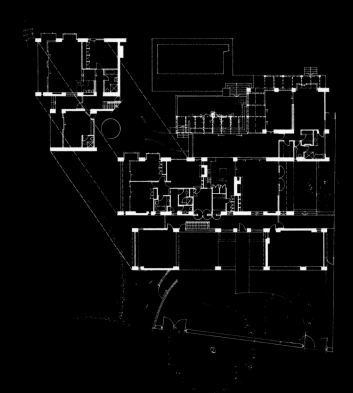

Norton Street Cinemas

Leichhardt
1993–1997

Located in the busy Italian stronghold of Leichhardt, the Norton Street Cinemas are a four-screen art house cinema complex, with a large book shop, restaurant and car parking, all fitted within a 1970s portal framed warehouse.

The design respects the ad-hoc manner in which Norton Street has developed, with a strong regional character and an intensity of commercial activity. An expressive functionalist approach was adopted, where the face of the building is composed from the uses found within. The tenancies push forward to display their contents to the street.

The composition is strengthened by the use of light to describe solid forms, with a backlit fibreglass parapet and a series of glowing fins over the entrance. The exterior appears both rugged and refined, a design strategy that was carried throughout the building to satisfy the limited budget. This approach also offered scope for purposeful detailing and higher levels of finish in critical public locations.

opposite
The main entry, with purpose-designed light fittings by Tim Greer.

right
The layered Norton Street elevation was added to the original warehouse building.

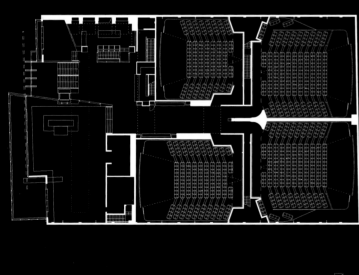

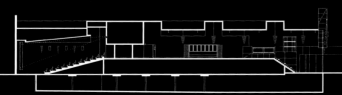

NORTON
STREET

CINEMA

NOW SHOWING

Actual size
of the next
really big
movie star.

shearer's on nort

music cafe books cyberca

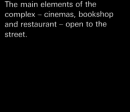

right
Main level plan.

below
The living areas surround a
sheltered deck.

opposite
The bedroom tower.

Whale Beach House

1996–1997

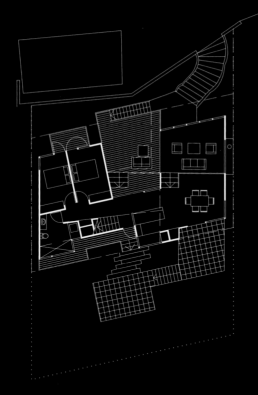

Perched on the edge of an escarpment looking northeast to the ocean, the house embraces the curve of Whale Beach and the distant headlands.

The house appears from street level as two towers linked by a sheltered entry deck and a modulating ground plane. Ascending the stairs, the scale of the building shifts to reveal two interlocking forms – one private and one public. The living areas pivot around the deck and are unified under a curved roof. This roof falls towards the view of the sea and rises to the hill behind, to create a dramatic relationship with the setting.

In contrast, the two-storey bedroom tower is a solid form expressing the smaller private spaces. It has an opposing rising roof that opens towards the view and allows intimacy in the more private spaces to the rear. The slatted timber base, between the ground and the main entry deck, anchors the house firmly to the site.

The house is entirely clad in durable hardwood, which has weathered to a soft grey. In the living room, the windows slide downwards so that the interior becomes an open verandah pavilion overlooking the sea.

Sydney Customs House

1995–1999

The refurbishment of the historic Customs House at Circular Quay was completed as the major tourism gateway to the City of Sydney prior to the Olympic Games. The six level building houses a variety of different cultural facilities including a city planning model, galleries, a museum, a number of bars and cafes and a restaurant. The project also includes major performance and exhibition spaces with specialised access and acoustic needs.

Customs House is a significant heritage building dating from 1845. It was built in successive stages in a variety of differing Classical styles, reaching its pre-renovation stage after the enclosure of its internal court in 1918. The significant 19th century sandstone fabric was extensively conserved, and unsympathetic additions removed to reveal as much as possible of the original courtyard space. The most important interior spaces were also restored, while other areas were left flexibly serviced for a variety of future cultural uses.

Escalators and new glass lifts created a vertical public promenade, catching unexpected views of the surrounding city through the fully-glazed new south wall.

The high level of energy-efficient, environmentally-sustainable design achieved for Customs House is unusual for a heritage refurbishment project. The design integrates sophisticated mechanical, lighting and solar control systems to enable virtually the whole building to be naturally ventilated and naturally lit.

The glass roof, floating above the upper levels, brings light deep into the six storey atrium. Layered glass solar-control blades track the sun throughout the day and year, reacting to overcast and night-time conditions.

A significant element of the project was the reworking of the Customs House Square. This was the location of the pre–1848 shoreline of Sydney Cove, where European settlers first landed in Aus-

left
Layered glass louvres over the suspended glass roof track the movement of the sun to control light and glare.

above
The rooftop addition replaces a 1940s caretaker's flat.

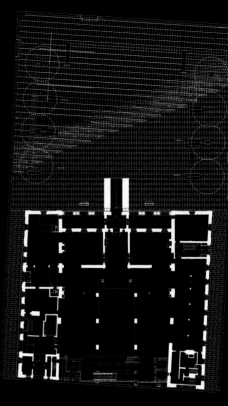

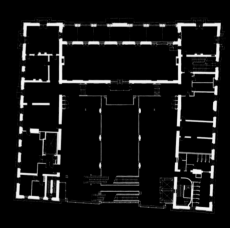

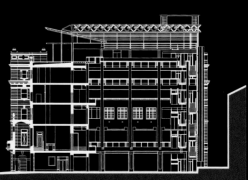

above
The 1914 lightwell has been
enclosed to form a new
atrium with celebrated vertical
circulation.

above right
Ground floor plan showing the
new Customs House Square.

centre right
First floor plan.

right
Section.

Tonkin Zulaikha Greer worked with the Hargreaves Associates' Masterplan for the Olympic Plaza to design the Lighting Towers for the Sydney 2000 Olympic Games. The 1.6 km long Olympic Plaza is the centre of the open space network of the Olympic site and provides access to the main stadium, railway station, indoor stadium and small halls.

The Towers are a series of 19 pylons, each 30 metres tall, which unite many functions on a very small footprint to facilitate crowd flows. Large-scale photovoltaic solar collection is coupled with sophisticated lighting and structure to create functional public sculpture. At their base, the Towers house all the services required for events in the Plaza, including high and low voltage power, communications, water and drainage.

A five metre square facetted mirror, designed with Barry Webb and Associates, has sophisticated photometrics, which reflect area lighting indirectly onto the Plaza, providing a unique, glare-free night-time ambience. 1150 square metres of photovoltaic collectors are arranged 6 metres above the paving, to provide areas of shade in the Plaza at key locations. These dramatic floating louvred shades are self-coloured and have been designed to provide easy event and maintenance access. At the time of completion, the photovoltaics provided one of the largest public solar collectors in the world, and continue to generate a net surplus of power.

The Towers have precast concrete bases, providing volumes to house services and seating. The shafts are angled to true north, away from the large masses of the stadia and towards the Olympic Boulevard, uniting the separate Towers into a cohesive group.

left
Cantilevered photovoltaic panels shade seating areas in the Olympic Plaza.

opposite
The Towers are angled to true north, and support facetted reflectors which provide glare-free reflected light.

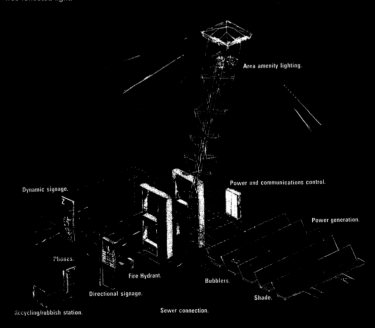

Area amenity lighting.

Dynamic signage.

Power and communications control.

Power generation.

Phones.

Fire Hydrant.

Bubblers.

Directional signage.

Shade.

Recycling/rubbish station.

Sewer connection.

Homebush Masterplan

Public Domain Paving, Signage, Street Furniture
and Lighting
1996–2003

Tonkin Zulaikha Greer, with a range of specialist sub-consultants, undertook the design, documentation and co-ordination of the Urban Elements for the 2000 Olympic Games site at Homebush Bay for the Olympic Coordination Authority. The Urban Elements – paving, signage, street furniture and lighting – represent a unifying and consistent fabric across all the precincts of this complex extended site.

The work, undertaken to strict timetables and under a rigorous environmental management plan, set new standards for accessibility and utilised leading Australian design and technology. The Elements include nine lighting pole types, ranging from modest pedestrian area lighting standards to large Olympic Plaza pylons, and twenty three styles and sizes of signs including way-finding and identification signage, with LED and other dynamic event markers. The street furniture includes bus and shade shelters, seating, bins, water fountains and bollards, and a palette of paving materials and types.

The different designs and the location strategies were fully specified in the Urban Elements Design Manual for use by the various precinct designers, and remains the standard for the on-going development of Sydney Olympic Park.

Tonkin Zulaikha Greer worked with Hargreaves Associates as Landscape and Master Planning consultants, The NSW Government Architect's Design Directorate, Barry Webb and Associates (Lighting), Hassell (Paving), KWA Design (Industrial Design) and Emery Vincent (Graphics).

left
The repeated forms of the towers and their massive bases unite to form a vast public verandah along the Olympic Plaza.

below
The various elements – shelters, lighting, signs, form a cohesive group with a defined character.

below right
Design drawing of the group of elements.

Fox Studios Retail Buildings

Paddington
1997–2000

The new Fox Studios use the heritage-listed former Sydney Showgrounds for film production studios, entertainment and retail spaces, with a combination of new and refurbished buildings. This project was developed within an overall master plan, conceived in liaison with government and community groups.

Four newly built two storey retail buildings by Tonkin Zulaikha Greer surround the major open space of the Showgrounds' former Parade Ring. They replace demolished mid 20th Century grandstands, and have been designed to address both the Ring and the new curving pedestrian street located behind them. The new buildings accommodate a mix of restaurant and general retail, and integrate with large areas of public open space. The forms of the buildings relate to the adjoining historic grandstands, and to the pedestrian routes that have been retained or created on the site.

The single-pitch and curved rooflines respond to the arc of the pedestrian street. The end elevations are modulated to create, between each of the buildings, a range of smaller open spaces. Details and materials – metal, face brick, timber – were developed to continue the spirit of the old Showground in a contemporary way.

opposite
The convex façade defines the main pedestrian street.

right
Between each of the four buildings are small clearly defined open spaces.

below right
A variety of curved forms face the Parade Ring of the former Showgrounds.

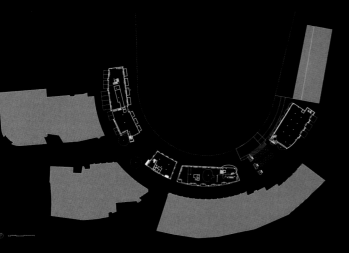

Designed for informal living, the house is located on the southern peninsula of Pearl Beach, north of Sydney, and enjoys sweeping views of the beach through a stand of eucalyptus trees.

A retreat for a family that is in a transitional move away from their city home, the house has been designed as two adjoining gabled pavilions, both constructed on a solid brick base with lighter timber and glass elements above. The interior has a flow of space from the upper level entrance to the ground level, where the living rooms open to the view and the sun.

above
East elevation.

left
Ground floor plan.

below
The north elevation overlooks the length of the beach.

opposite
The living, dining and kitchen areas open onto the sheltered deck.

Australian Pavilion

World Expo 2000
Hannover Germany

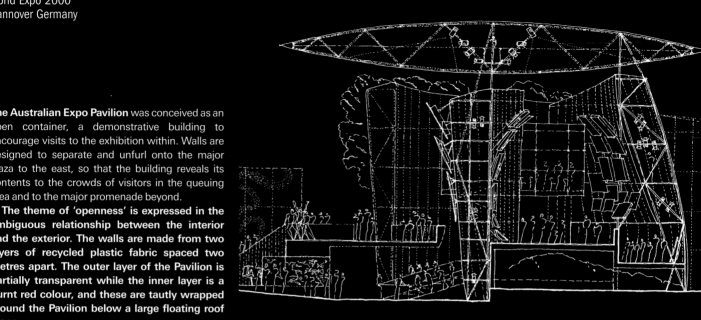

The Australian Expo Pavilion was conceived as an open container, a demonstrative building to encourage visits to the exhibition within. Walls are designed to separate and unfurl onto the major plaza to the east, so that the building reveals its contents to the crowds of visitors in the queuing area and to the major promenade beyond.

The theme of 'openness' is expressed in the ambiguous relationship between the interior and the exterior. The walls are made from two layers of recycled plastic fabric spaced two metres apart. The outer layer of the Pavilion is partially transparent while the inner layer is a burnt red colour, and these are tautly wrapped around the Pavilion below a large floating roof plane.

Exhibition displays shift in and out of the space between the two layers of wall, which symbolically identify the mobility and transparency of the Australian political, social and geographical landscape. The roof, a 'thermal pillow', floats like a giant screen above the Pavilion. Illuminated from the walls below, it displays different configurations of light and colours throughout day and night.

The Australian Pavilion is a sustainable building. It was made from temporary materials such as fabric and standard prefabricated steel elements, which were all re-used on its removal at the close of Expo 2000.

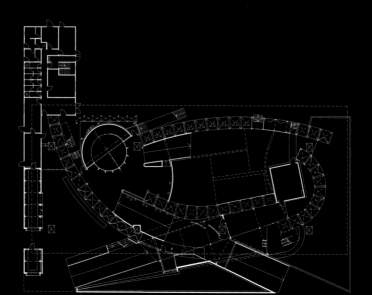

above
Section of the pavilion.

left
Entry level plan.

opposite
The external walls are lay
of recycled plastic fabric.

The structure of the pavilion comprised standard stage-set components, entirely reused after Expo.

Peace Pavilion

Centennial Park
2000

below left
Plan.

right
The Pavilion gestures to the
landscape and the sky.

A low-cost demountable structure, which was temporarily located in Centennial Park as a millennium gift to Sydney and NSW from the Brahma Kumaris Yoga Centres Incorporated. It has since been re-erected elsewhere.

Looking north across the Duck Pond of Centennial Park, the pavilion has an exhibition area and a meditation space. The floor level is set above the grass plane to form a generous seat in the park. Supported by a steel structure, the floor and roof have each been developed as timber 'leaves' held apart by translucent resin and weathered steel pods which present texts and dedications. The roof is a multiple layering of timber screening and translucent sheeting, casting reflective shadows across the timber planes and vertical surfaces of the Pavilion.

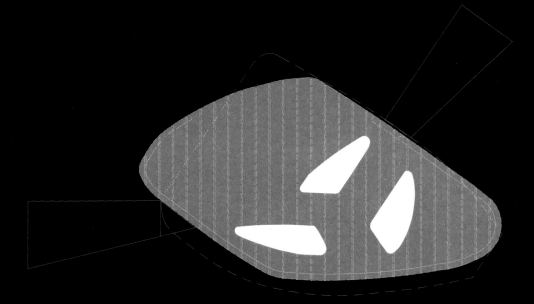

Bellevue Hill Apartments

2000–2001

Located in a constricted commercial setting with excellent westward views over parkland to the city, the building has six apartments on three storeys, with retail on the ground floor.

The new building facilitates a transition between the differing scales of the two neighbouring buildings, sensitively integrating a contemporary structure into a complex and established streetscape. The apartments are arranged to maximise views and privacy, and each apartment runs through the depth of the building to provide cross ventilation. The landscaped roof of the carpark enhances the outlook to the north.

The building was constructed efficiently with straightforward detailing, and develops the logic of simple precast concrete construction. It capitalises upon the raw expressive combination of natural materials and a simple bold form, with high-quality internal finishes.

opposite
The east elevation overlooks a pool on the roof of the garage.

right
The access stair utilizes a hard-edged industrial range of materials.

below
Typical floor plan.

A six storey apartment building designed to integrate with the streetscape and existing qualities of Australia's densest residential precinct. The six apartments, with retail on the ground floor, are arranged not only to maximise views, cross ventilation and privacy but also to generate a form that acts as a transition of scale between two neighbouring historic buildings.

The façade, which can be likened to a mask, is clad in thin copper tiles, which will acquire a patina over time. The double-height apartments have steel bridges connecting the second bedroom with an outdoor balcony, and full-height garage-style operable glass doors provide a valuable extension of the interior to the north. A rooftop glass pavilion accommodates a penthouse.

left
The double height apartments have power-operated glass doors to open the entire space to the north.

below
Section.

opposite
The south façade, partly clad in copper: a contemporary infill in an historic setting.

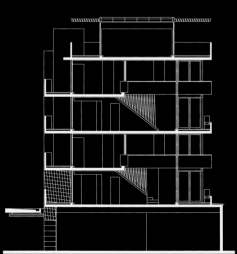

Killcare House

1998–2000

A beach house that deliberately feels like the beach – open, unforced, a true shift from the city – for shared use by two families.

The scheme develops as a tall timber-framed 'castle', piled up along a straight stair. Its robust forms are cantilevered and interlocking, sheltered under a single plane of roof whose slope matches the tree canopy. The plan inflects to retain huge sandstone boulders, which stabilise and define the steep site. The building's junction with the ground is carefully controlled to respect the fragile surface of the 45° slope and remnant lush bushland. An earlier garage and studio on the street frontage were reconstructed to conform with the architecture of the main house.

A restrained palette of surfaces and detail has been selected with long-life, simple materials: treated timber poles, durable hardwood, zinc, with unpainted fibre cement walls, roof, gutters, and ceilings. All will relax, grey and uncoated, into the bush setting.

Every room sees the surf; every room is private yet connected; every room has a different height and aspect, with a different view of the bush. The kitchen is a bridge and a link – the heart of the house.

The structure is celebrated, allowed to be separate from the simple walls and partitions. Windows occur only where they are needed. The conserved natural rock outcrops on the site join with the architecture to form exterior 'rooms'.

The project was designed by Tonkin Zulaikha Greer with Ellen Woolley.

top right
Main level plan.

centre right
Top level (left) and lower levels
(right).

right
North elevation, clearly
showing the very steep site.

opposite
The exterior is clad in
unpainted fibre cement sheet.

Under the single pitch of the roof, spaces vary in height.

Sir Henry Parkes Memorial School of Arts

Tenterfield
2000–2001

Tenterfield is located high in the Great Dividing Range in far northern NSW. The School of Arts is a complex of buildings built in seven stages, the earliest dating from 1870. Sir Henry Parkes, then Premier of NSW, delivered the famous 'Tenterfield Oration' in the Original Hall in 1889, one of the key events leading to the 1901 Federation of the Australian States. The building is also significant in that it was the first property acquired by the National Trust in NSW.

As part of the Centenary of Federation, the School of Arts has been conserved, refurbished and extended. The project includes a range of cultural and community facilities for the town of Tenterfield. A new library occupies the 1912 Billiard Room, and includes a new wing accommodating the library book-stacks and offices. A 250 seat theatre and foyer, with full backstage facilities, is formed around the 1902 Boer War Memorial Hall. The focus of the complex is the Henry Parkes and Federation Museum in the Original Hall and reading rooms.

The design articulates and functionally unifies the seven construction stages grouped around a sheltered central courtyard. The use of local red brick and the scale of the projecting bay windows unite the varied roof forms of the new and heritage buildings. The School of Arts is the focus for historical and cultural activity within the Tenterfield region and played a major role in the Centenary of Federation celebrations.

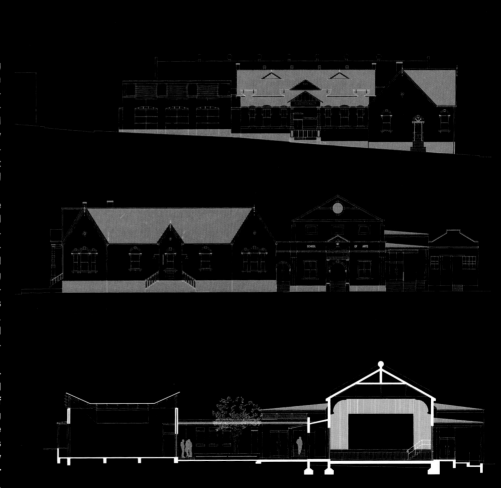

above
The Sir Henry Parkes Room contains artefacts, including a portrait bust.

opposite
The new wing and the 1912 Billiard Room form the community library.

The Darlington Centre

The University of Sydney
1999–2002

The core of this project is an intact 1880s house
formerly the Director's Residence for the adjacer
former Blind Institute. The Darlington Centr
accommodates new conference, function an
dining facilities for the University of Sydney.

**The house itself has been conserved an
adapted as lounge areas, office and small mee
ing rooms. The major spaces of the Centre ar
accommodated in a new addition, designed a
two wings on a single-level. The clear separa
tion of the three main building forms, articu
lated with landscaped courts, is in accordanc
with the conservation plan and provides
sense of openness and light.**

One wing, a masonry structure, has twin adap
able meeting rooms, a catering kitchen and ba
The other, designed as a lightweight, steel-frame
garden pavilion, is a 150 seat dining room. Define
by an internal floating curved timber canopy, th
dining room opens to the northern verandah ar
gardens beyond. The simple steel and glass arch
tecture of this new pavilion contrasts with th
enclosed masonry of the old house.

The existing garden areas have been reworked
provide suitable exterior spaces for functions, ar
twelve 19th Century stone gateposts, excavate
from the site, define the generous lawns.

above left
The dining room is conceived
as an open garden pavilion.

left
The curved timber ceiling
defines the dining and
function room.

above
The main pavilion opens north
onto a sheltered lawn.

right
Plan.

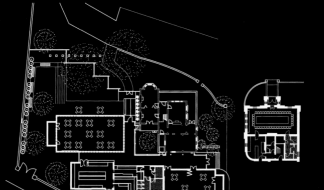

Putney House

1999–2001

On the northern bank of the Parramatta River, the site is set between large new architecturally undistinguished houses. The view is to the south, and the plan was designed to take the form of an enclosed and private north-facing courtyard with living rooms extending through the depth of the house.

The main living space is double-height. The expressive form of its folded plywood roof reaches through the wall to form a sunshade for its exposed glazing. On the upper floor, the main bedrooms and study are reached from a gallery bridge across this space.

Externally the house has a dual character – to the north and facing the courtyard, the forms are playful and expressive, while the southern riverfront elevation recalls a pure ideal of the classical villa, with three pavilions raised on a blank base. The external walls are grey-stained ply, jointed with aluminium tee sections. Windows and solid shutters slide across the face of the walls, to leave the openings free of framing.

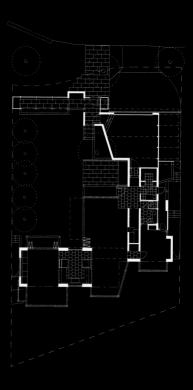

left
The south façade, which looks out over the Parramatta River.

right
Ground floor plan.

above
Living rooms open to the
northern court and to the river
to the south.

left
The folded ceiling of the living
room extends through the
glass as a sunshade.

opposite
External walls are grey-stained
plywood with aluminium
jointing strips.

National Gallery of Australia

2000-2003

Tonkin Zulaikha Greer's involvement with this project commenced with the development of a 25 year master plan for the National Gallery of Australia / High Court 'Campus' of the Parliamentary Triangle in Canberra. The on-going development of the Campus was planned to include sites for major new arts and government buildings, integrated pedestrian access, parking and servicing, and the creation of a significant and defined central Campus Square. Of major importance to the study was the conservation and development of the nationally-significant landscaping of the precinct.

The Campus Square was developed as a large triangular entry court with an ecological water garden. Designed with Hargreaves Associates, the integrated landscape provided a new major approach to the building from Canberra's 'cultural mall', King Edward Terrace, and the conservation and completion of Harry Howard's wonderful 1970s Sculpture Garden.

Several approaches to a planned 25 year redevelopment of the Gallery building were developed. The focus of this work was a reconstruction of the 'front door' of the building, where the abandonment of the 1960s urban planning had compromised the arrival sequence. New southern foyers and comprehensible vertical circulation were required to access all of the building's spaces. The new work was developed to respect the significant qualities of this major Brutalist landmark, whilst overcoming identified shortcomings in its entry sequence, visitor orientation and circulation. New education and service spaces as well as major new galleries were planned.

At competition stage, a glass 'sliver' was inserted adjacent to the existing portico to contain new escalators and foyers. Following Tonkin Zulaikha Greer's success in this competition, and in response to a briefing by the National Gallery of Australia, the planned new foyer was greatly enlarged to enclose a six-storey high daylit glass atrium, creating the central event and orientation space which the building lacked. Sophisticated multi-layered sculptural glass façades were engineered to pre-condition outside air, buffer day/night temperature changes and control sunlight.

This scheme was abandoned due to moral rights issues.

Subsequent schemes by Tonkin Zulaikha Greer moved the new entry away from the sensitive south-west corner elevation to face directly onto King Edward Terrace. Sculpted zinc-clad fins responded to the solidity of the original bush-hammered off-form concrete, and provided dual entrances to a single extended foyer space with focus galleries above.

Work by Tonkin Zulaikha Greer was suspended to allow resolution of the moral rights of the original architect, Edwards Madigan Torzillo and Briggs.

Completed parts of the project include the refurbishment of many of the main galleries, including the 17m tall Gallery 2, and the replacement of failed sunshading, windows and services. The approach to the interior work was to remove as much of the unsympathetic later 'layers' as possible, maintaining hanging space but revealing the original concrete architecture. Particular care was taken to remove intrusive cladding and dropped ceilings, which hid sculptural junctions and connections, as well as to restore the building's heroic scale and to open up significant vistas through the linked gallery and ramp spaces.

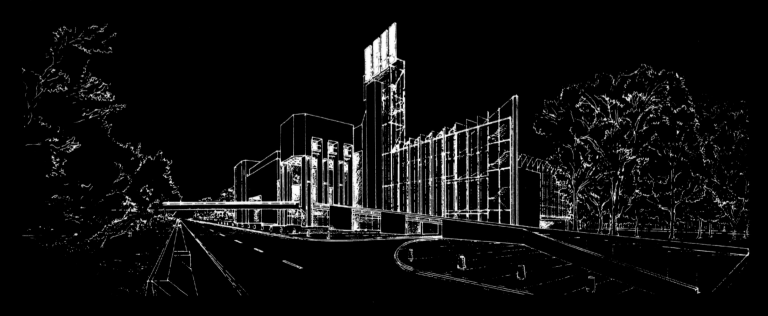

left
The competition-winning
scheme developed the idea of
a thin glass-enclosed addition
housing vertical circulation,
linked to the existing entry
foyer and portico.

above
As the design developed, the
addition became a major new
6 storey foyer, linking all of
the Gallery's complex levels.

Centric Apartments

Victoria Park, Sydney
2000–2002

47 apartments and 16 townhouses were developed as the model first stage for the development of an entire inner city district. Victoria Park will eventually accommodate over 3000 residents, and is being built on the site of a disused factory complex, once a racecourse, on the southern fringe of Sydney.

Designed in collaboration with LFA Pacific Architects, the development completely occupies one new urban block and creates a dense urban environment, where each of the apartments and townhouses has excellent solar access, privacy and a green outlook. Roof terraces capture broad views to the city skyline.

Each of the four façades responds to its orientation and setting. The north elevation opens onto the adjoining parkland, while the west is clad in cobalt brickwork and creates a micro environment with the avenue of dense fig trees lining the adjoining boulevard.

Balconies on this side have contrasting yellow soffits, and project into the tree canopies. The east and south are cubist developments of the internal program and are less expressive, in response to the more enclosed residential streets. The four wings, with basement car parking, surround a private green court.

above
A row of three-storey townhouses faces north onto a small park.

right
The curved west façade of the apartments is faced with cobalt glazed brick.

far right
Ground floor plan.

opposite
Apartment balconies look into the fig trees lining Joynton Avenue

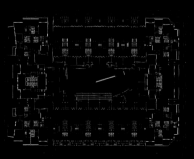

Lilyfield House

2000–2001

Designed by Ellen Woolley and Peter Tonkin, this house occupies a constrained site in a built-up nineteenth-century inner-Sydney suburb, although the 191 square metre site had never been developed. The extensive sandstone outcrops and a major cross-fall presented a significant challenge to create a dwelling, which would provide acceptable levels of solar access and privacy, whilst capturing the sweeping city views and separating the occupants from the traffic arteries to the south.

The house is developed from a strong southern street wall of glazed brick with an inbuilt pattern in two shades of black. This three-storey wall is a gesture to the public, an abstracted billboard and a rampart, as well as a reference to the vanishing industrial heritage of the area. Internally, circulation is in a one metre zone along this wall and is defined by thick masonry walls, articulated to form cupboards and lighting recesses.

Light is brought into the lower levels of this zone through a clerestory window that captures the northern sun. The circulation zone extends beyond the house as a floating timber entry bridge and a small upper-level balcony.

The northern part of the house accommodates the living spaces and bedrooms, and is expressively timber framed, scaled and detailed to sympathise with the adjoining small Victorian houses. The end elevations open to the views: east to the dramatic city skyline, and west to a small forest of eucalypts on the site's rocky outcrop.

The house has carefully resolved active and passive ESD systems, including enhanced natural ventilation with clerestory 'breeze catchers', heat pump in-floor heating and cooling, and computer-modelled sun shading. Low-energy and recycled natural materials are used throughout, with a minimum of applied finishes.

left
The western elevation relates to the scale of the adjoining cottages.

below
Section and south elevation.

opposite
The southern street wall forms a 'defence' against an adjoining busy transport corridor.

The circulation zone allows a
wash of northern light down
the entire height of the house.

above
A 'carpet' of timber flows through the circulation zone of the house.

left
Storage and services are housed in the thickened wall to the circulation zone.

Two shades of black glazed
brick form an urban-scaled
artwork.

Pavilions on the Bay

Blackwattle Bay, Glebe
1998–2001

Pavilions on the Bay is a nine storey group of 46 waterfront apartments, built as two wings. The taller wing directly addresses Glebe Point Road, forming an articulate streetscape edge to this broad avenue of Victorian houses and shops, while the lower eastern pavilion mediates the scale of the development to the harbour-side public park. The project relates both to Glebe's heritage precinct and to Sydney Harbour, creating a significant new waterfront public space and a sizeable interior courtyard area for the use of residents.

Materials – sandstone, copper, concrete, brickwork and timber – were selected to preserve the memory of the site's former timber industrial buildings. The new structure is built using reinforced concrete, externally expressed as an articulated framework to identify the various apartments. Sandstone is used to create street and garden walls.

Each apartment has a defined and individual plan, with extensive private outdoor space and generous indoor accommodation. Living spaces, both indoor and outdoor, are developed as glass or open pavilions floating in shallow pools, which articulate their volumes and visually connect the apartments with the expanse of the harbour.

left
The south western elevation on Glebe Point Road, is a series of pavilions and glazed entries, scaled to reflect the neighbouring Victorian architecture.

below
Entry level plan.

opposite
The building unites masonry forms with elements in natural copper, stone and timber.

following spread
View over Blackwattle Bay to the apartments.

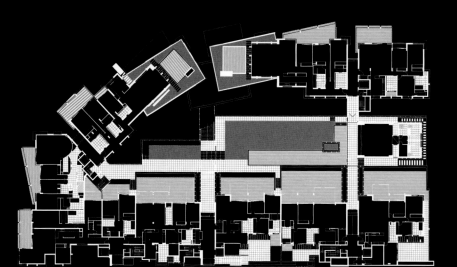

opposite
North eastern elevation of the
main wing, overlooking a
series of pools.

above right
Eastern wing penthouse
apartment and terrace
overlooking Blackwattle Bay.

right
View up Glebe Point Road

left
The model from the south.

bottom left
Ground floor plan.

bottom right
Typical silo apartment plan.

Silos Apartment Project

Newtown
1999–2005

The Crago Mill in Newtown, on the western fringe of Sydney's inner city, has landmark structures that are significant heritage survivors of a period when flour milling was dominated by large city mills alongside railway lines.

The concrete silos and a tall complex of timber storage bins were originally used for the storage of grain. This project converts these structures into residential use with associated open space. A new lower-rise structure provides additional apartments alongside the refurbished heritage buildings. All new work is clearly articulated, and the retained portions will be restored in such a way that the three buildings form a coherent and functional whole.

The project has been developed to retain the industrial qualities, scale and aesthetics of the existing complex. The three buildings will accommodate 59 apartments over 14 levels. The existing ground-level bases of the historic silos and bins have architecturally impressive timber and concrete structural forms, and have been designed as the two main foyers for the new building. At the top of the silos, a new three-storey metal-clad 'crown' provides penthouse accommodation.

The Silo apartments take advantage of the circular plan forms to create unusual but rational room shapes, reconciling southern views with northern sunlight access. Throughout the development, original unfinished wall surfaces have been retained, linking the past to the building's present use.

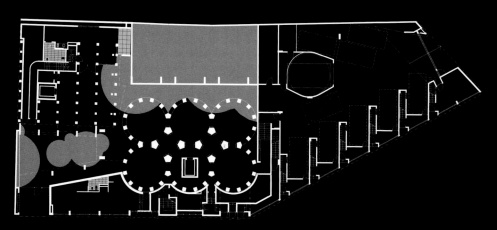

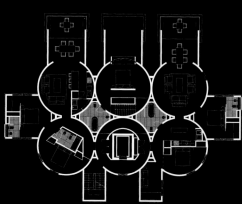

The Australian War Memorial

London
2002–2003

Tonkin Zulaikha Greer, in collaboration with the artist Janet Laurence, won this project through a limited competition conducted by the Australian Government. The Memorial is located on a prominent site in cental London, and commemorates the efforts of the Australian Services, allied with those of Great Britain, in the two World Wars. One hundred thousand Australians fighting "in defence of freedom" were killed alongside the British during these battles.

The site, at Hyde Park Corner, is at the fulcrum of the ceremonial route through London and is shared with the Wellington Arch and the Ionic Screen by Decimus Burton, both classical 18th Century monuments by Decimus Burton, built from Portland stone. The Australian Memorial unites the green space at this critical intersection, and has been designed as a respectful gesture to both the existing historic monuments and the eloquent landform itself.

The wall of the Memorial encloses the site's sloping grassed amphitheatre and creates a focal space, both for quiet reflection and for major commemorative events. The curved sculptural wall is entirely faced with prefabricated green granite from Western Australia. Each stone was prefabricated to exacting tolerances in Australia and site-fixed in a very short period, many to complex laser-cut stainless steel cradles.

The Memorial's iconography is key to the symbolism of the design, and comprises a layering of two sets of texts – the larger letters are formed by 'bolding' the smaller type, a method designed to emphasise the relationship of the individual to the vider forces of war and society. The smaller typeface lists 24,000 towns, the birthplaces of the Australian service men and women. Significantly, many of these places are in the UK or Europe, and several are repeated in the larger text type. The places named in the larger text are a selection of 47 significant battlegrounds where the Australians fought alongside the British.

A major water feature was a requirement of the brief, and this has been designed as a random wash of water over successive panels of text, symbolically refreshing memories and cleansing the pain of suffering and loss. The Memorial was designed and constructed in under twelve months, and was dedicated by HM the Queen and by the Australian and British Prime Ministers on Remembrance Day, 2003.

The curved form of the Memorial shelters a place of quiet reflection.

left
A random wash of water
flows over the inscribed
names.

above
The dedication ceremony on
11 November 2003, the 75th
anniversary of the World War I
Armistice.

following pages
The small names are of the
24,000 towns where the
Australian service people were
born, and emboldened they
spell out 47 of the major
battles of the two World
Wars.

FIELDS HEATHERBRAE GUNDOWRING WESTERN HAINAULI WALMER DENICULL CREEK
ETAPLES COLLARENE OTTERY LEWIS PONDS RORKES DRIFT WALLAMBAH SHIPHAM HILLSBOROUGH
RE MYLA CLAUDE ROAD ONGA CARRENDALE COTTEE KELLINGWORTH HEADCORN NE
BACK YAMM WEST COOLUP LAGOON CREEK KANGAROO JINJA MCINTYRES FY
ARAGON BLACKWARRY WEDDERBURN BREMER MORRISONS MURRAH AHO CUDD
BOISA LOCKLEIGH KALARAH MILAN TOTTON LLANGEINOR DAGLISH URADU GLENROCK
REHAU LILSNE WARRIMOO LANGHOLM DULVERTON RABE BOOGARDIE A
MANGANA CARPENTER UPPINGHAM
BROULEE PENICUIK BARROW IN FURNESS LAXTON PULHAM IMMARNA SWAN CREEK WYNARKA
PARK BEYROUT H KANGAROO GROUNDS BOONAL RANELAGH NEEDILUP ESK VALE WANOURI
LLANDUDWEN NARAN BULLYARD MURCHISON WALKDEN REEDY
MAYANUP BEVERLY MIDDLESBORO KROSNO MOONBAH LONGERENONG MOORA
KINGTON ALVESTON WYLIES FLAT ARMATREE GOGANGO HOLLINWOOD KINTORE TONBRIDG
LYNNE KIRKBY LONSDALE DINOGA CUNJURONG KINGS CROSS SOUTH BOULDER URLI
PARAP DAMPIER BINGLEBURRA CASNIGO AURONZO TELANGATUK ALOE WEETANGI
OUGH WYENA VALENCIA RUABON MITCHELL HILL WAGSTAFF BOTE
MOUNT MORRISTON KOLANEC YOUNGERINA OAKPARK TILBURG BENA MAYVILLE ILLALONG C
ALE DEIN MANNANARIE SAN MARIA DOTSWOOD WOONGARRA
BRIGGS BARNA SHARROW NORFOLK ISLAND KANYAN ELLONG TABARA THOUROUT
UDDIE MULWALA WARTHA BRITANNIA CREEK LEITHOLM STEPAN BIRA BIRA LAKEFIELD
SAVANAKA CLIFDEN SOMERS AGHADA MUKDEN WANDANA BARREN ISLAND
KANAVA KIAORA BUNDOORA KNIGHTSTOWN BLYTHE HEADS BEENAK HEMM
GUYARRE BOROUGH HUTS BARRYS REEF BROUGHTY FERRY SCOTBY FOSTERTON
CANAWINDRA GREAT MALVERN SIDONIA LONG PLAIN DOG HOLES EAST PRESTON STETOVI
HOLLAND'S LANDING JUGIONG QUANDONG COOLAMBIL STANNINGTON CARCOAR
MOUNT BARKER IRVINESTOWN WANG WAUK BATLO SALERNO WONWONDAH THE GINGHET WARRABEE
PALAMOS WILSONS VALLEY TANBAN LINCON YOLLA PUMPHERSTON BAERAMI CREEK BENTLY
KIRKALDY KUOPIO TIMMSVALE SKILLY ORU ROSS HILL HOFFMAN THURGOONA FISHERMENS BEN
COLIBAN FAULDHOUSE SINGEN TOKOMARU BAY GERMANTOWN COORABELL MONGO YALLAH
BILBUL KINGSKETTLE POOLAIJELO ANSWER DOWNS DHORA WINCHENDON VALE MOUNT EL
PINKERTON TIBBERMORE KOGRI GANOO GANOO STRATHBLANE ISLE OF WIGHT NORTH DORRIGO
S CAMURRA SOMMERTON VRBNIK ABBOTS LACHLANS PARK GLASSTON BRAMBLE K
BESSIEBELLE GOORGANGA PONDICHERRY BURNEWANG PHEASANT CREEK PARKES FALKENHAGEN
LAKE PLAIN LOCHARBRIGGS DIGGERS REST LIMONITE KOOKABOOKRA CREEK JUNCTION NARELLAN
GRASS VALLEY RIVERSDALE SPEARWOOD LOWER TARWIN AUGUSTUS DOWNS BOOUBYJAN MARELLA
WABDALLAH CROMARTY NOOJEE EPPALOCK NEW WELL CANNINGTON CHINLEY GLEN
CH MULBEN KOWLOON GREENMOUNT CHAPELLE BORUGASUSU BARKERS CREEK
CARBEAN HARLESTONE MANANA DANTUTU ROXBOROUGH MURRADOC SAINT-FE
FIELD COW FLAT RODHAM STONEYCROFT MONTENEGRO BOSWORTH PYRAMID HILL LAKE M
MERLIN AITAPE GLENLEITH ELSINORE STROOD LEXTON MANGERTON HARRIEDALE
WEST DEAN JENNAPULLIN BOROGOMARRA WARRANANGA CAMBRIAN HILL
ESPINOSA DE CERRATO EAGLEBY O'OKIEP HOLIAROOVSK DINNINGTON FERNMOUNT BAMGANIE
PAYWIT MEARE HALKIRK ASMARA SEASPRAY CAIRNBROOK
SVENDBORG LOWER CHITTERING BERESFIELD CROCODILE WIRRILLA BIG SWAMP
O WALLSALL CARPENTARIA DOWNS GOLBORNE GLENDALE NARRE WARREN BRITISH COCHIN M
BELLE VUE ABY KIRKMAIDEN RUBYVALE WISLEY COOLUP TRINITY BEACH
WANGRABELLE TROWBRIDGE KALABAGH DUNNSVILLE TOOGONG DUMAR OAK
ARRANGOBILLY COOMBES KAWANA MEPPADI ALECTOWN ALDRINGHAM MEMPHIS
BA WELLINGTON JENOLAN CAVES WANDERA HALDON KAARIMBA PALM GROVE
NOR ROSTREVOR WINTERBOURNE URALLA WARRAMBOO NERIMBERA CABRAMATTA
ZAANDAM ELLENGOWAN TEA TREE GULLY PENNINGTON GOWANGARDIE
A PARK TOMEWIN CASULA TRENCIN NORTH ELMHAM MOORELANDS MYRTLEFORD FAIR VIEW
MONK FRYSTON CHORLEYWOOD PROSPECT HILL LIMBURG MERRILL ASHTON UNDER HIL
ELENA CHANTILLY BROKE WOODY POINT CHEDBURGH WALLARAH MASSIE HAVANT
SOUTH HUMMOCKS CARRUM CUST GLENMORRISTON PORT ELIZABETH SHACKLETON BUCKAJO
PEKOI ENNISKILLEN DONGON PLAIN BASILDON EVANDALE BURTON MALEA BURRANGON
ORALVILLE MONTE MAGNO PALGARUP SANDY BEACH KOORT KOORT NONG LOWER CREEK NEWBUR
ULGAWARRINA OSA ROCKVALE SAVANNE GYMPIE BYRRILL CREEK CARDIFF
WEILHEIM COWAL WILCANNIA PIMPINIO NORTH WILLOUGHBY WARRENTINNA EAST GUYONG
DEDERANG BISHOPSTONE SHELLEY BEACH WELBECK FOX HILL ESBJERG WESTLAKE BRACKENRIDGE
VERMONT HILL SPRING PLAINS CORFE CASTLE NARACOOPA RISALPUR PORT FRANKLIN
TOOGOOLAWAH NONOPAI PETFORD VALOKA NATTE YALLOCK BALTRAY DOWN
URG MOUNT HAWTHORN COOLRINGDON CLIVE BIRCHGROVE DUNEDIN NYAM
EUNGAI RAIL ARBROATH MANNINGTREE BARATTA PATANGA
CRAVENSVILLE MIDSOMER NORTON MUNGHORN WOOLERINA BIERBANK SMITHS CREEK
NT WARWICK OLD MILL CLOUGH EDEN VIEW TYNONG GREENBUSHES HOOD RIVER
DUMBARTON TOWIGON GRANGE TAMBAR SPRINGS APPLEBY BUFFALO RIVER TALGAI TOMICH
STER MCCRAE DAVIOT PENDLETON USWORTH HOWLONG
BLACKBUTT TICHBORNE JINGERA ELIZABETH PARK ENGLEWOO
WOOTONG VALE PIRIES RABATO LOWER BARRINGTON DARGIN
MAR DEL PLATA KILLUCAN HAYSTACK STAINFORTH WAHLEN MILLEWA BARBERTON NORTH

SWATON LUCA HARLEY HARRISFIELD HARE MOUNT RICHMOND ROSNY HOLLY DOWNS CUDGEWA
BLACKAWTON LODA BURES KOORALLA INGERSOLL BRAYTON NORTH ARAMARA MUMMEL GORLITZ
NIAGARA MORTLAKE SUNNYDALE WILLOW GREEN TRIABUNNA NORTH BARHAM RONLAND D
NORTH KENSINGTON KIRUP NORTON-ON-TEES CRYSTALBROOK HAILSHAM LOSSIEMOUTH BATHWIC
ON WEDGEWOOD SOUTH BRISBANE TETU BOW PARK OAKLY VIENA ESSENDEAN L
CARSINGTON CHERRYUP GOULBURN WEIR TULLYNESSLE ANDREWS TOWALLUM GOYURA BALLYCLARE
POINT CLARE KILMANAGH YANGET SAINT PETERSBURG VILLIERSTOWN PORTH ABERCORN
RAYLTON ROGANS HILL TALAROOK RYDALMERE KURIDALA STOURBRIDGE JANNALI WESTHAVEN LOCHBUIE
RUTLAND PLAINS JEW FISH POINT LUZERNE NAZARETH WHARMINDA JAUNTER MINGELO
KILKELL KILKENNY BODFARI LESTER BUNYARRA FRANKLINFORD MEEANDAH CHILTERN
COONGULLA YANDINA HAZELWOOD STYX OPPMANNA PRETTY GULLY KINGHAM MELDRUM
HANDSWORTH WENSLEYDALE WORLE GOOLMANGAR HAMM BERKELEY WAREGEM WAL
ESMERE TERANG ADLINGTON NAVARA EAST POPANYINNING BRINDABELLA CLARKSTON UMI
BOWMANS BULGARY BEEVOR YARROW CREEK CAROONA COLEYVILLE ENGLISH T
LAMBERT TOOMPINE ELGIN VALE BOLWARRAH BRIDGE OF ALLAN POINT PASS CHI
PULTARA DALYUP APPLECROSS GRANGE SLAVGOROD FORDS TALDRA COC
CROOKSTON BANGAROO TATALA BOOLATHANA HOLLYWOOD MEIFOD
DEBORAH TARRANYURK ARSBECK BRANSCOMBE LOGAN DOWNS LANGAA
CUTTS CROSSING WILLOWMAVIN LINCOLN OLD BEACH BARRINGHA MICHLBACH
TTON LASCELLES WATH CHIPPENDALE WANDIN ROSENDALE STEINHORST WICKL
TOORUMBEE NORTH BALWYN ACKLAND CARTERTON NERRIGA MUDALL MEDBURY
ORD PEELWOOD PRUDHOE EURAH NEW LISKEARD HONOLULU BURNGUP YARRANLEA
UGI MAHRATTA DARGAVILLE WEST GRINSTEAD RAZAN BARRON MESSINO CLARINDA MONA VALE

LOWIE MARYAMMA OMAI MANGONUI STANBROOK LOCHGELLY LLANDILO BOONOKE MINGAY THUXT
ELELE KARE CACCIA MARYBOURGH WALTERHALL FOREST REEFS CARDIFF HEIGHTS DEZZO G
KOKI GWOZDZIEC BANANA HAYFORD RATHDOWNEY INCE NAIDIA DULBYDILLA TURINO
AREW PALAFRUGELL ADDLESTONE HALL NEW BARNET MOORABBIN YEALERING SYLVATERRE
REEDHAM PICKERING WALKERVILLE DOBO BLADON HENLEY BEACH NEWFOUNDLAND
ORE GROVE MOUNTRATH LINCOLNSHIRE DRAPERSTOWN GALWARY QUANGALLIN SAPPERTON MATAURA
RON DURRAN DURRA WANIGELA MURRINDAL GERANG GERUNG HANWOOD PATNA C
AMBIE WILBERTREE FLAT KIRRIBILLI KOKIRI COUTO PORT CLINTON VLADIVOSTOK BAROOL
FUNA THYLUNGRA CANNUM AUGUSTA MOORMBOOL GORE HILL TORRYBURN KIONION KA
TCHIE CORNALLA BAY OF PLENTY POONINDIE GLENGOWRIE KNEBSWORTH ELFIN WILGA HILL
Y MARKET DAGENHAM MONS WILLMOT DEPOT HILL NIMBY WINTERTON MURREE KENWYN
BAY WILLIAMTOWN CATERHAM OTAUTAU HALD MATAPUPU HEBDEN KILLARNEY VALE
WANURP UNDINA MARRAWING KUNDIP DENNIS WALKERTON TREGEAGLE VIZZINI W
DECO LATURA SINNA GROSSOTTO PARAGON LINTON TANNYMOREL ROWVILLE
GSTONE DIDCOT ROOSE PARKERVILLE HUMSHAUGH NEDLANDS MALAMO
GAMREE BONNIE HILLS KALABRA GOTTENBURG MANAM ISLAND DURHAM LEAD PIGGOREET
CUBALLING WAUNINGI MOORABINDA COLESBURG GUILDFORD ORMEAU YA
TERRIBLE VALE SAINT ANDREW BARRINE ANTIGUA ALTONA KLINCI
LE HAMILTON BROAD HINTON BELMONT PARK ARORA CONVOY LESTINE LANGHO
VILLE RIVERGLADE FOLKSTONE WARRAH RIDGE BLAKEHURST
CHERO STRAWBERRY SCHIO MARANOA MOONBI KINCHELA
BALD BLAIR PADTHAWAY FLINTON NORTH ROTHBURY CARDROSS YUROK
TON STRETFORD SWAMP OAK ERIE NARRIAH PROSPER DONALD
RLEY BEACONSFIELD ANGASTON KEMPTON MARSWORTH CLYNNOG-FAWR SCOTTSDALE
OTA I FERN BANK COLBINABBIN MARRAN EAST BUDLEIGH CURRAJONG G
ORDESLE CHIGWELL YOUNDEGIN JINGHI HERTFORD YARRUNGA
ERRAMUNGUP CHARLOTTENBERG UNDERDALE GROHOTE PINNACLE VYCHAN R
KAI RAVI NASIK ROUMALLA COBAW GRANARD BUTMAROO VERDUN DJU
MARCU HILL OZORKOW MOOTAI SAINT PETERS ROWE LLANNOR
NUTFIELD BURRINGTON WILDCROFT THREE SPRINGS KARRAMOMUS CARRATHOOL BOONG
MIDHURST NORTH DENILIQUIN CARAGABAL ABRAM BALINTORE MOUNT CROSBY YAM
HOLLOW TREE GODSTONE NOMOTA DUNGAY ADELAIDE LEAD CARY BAY
MACQUARIE FIELDS CRUMLIN NARLOO BONNYVIEW WOODFORD GREEN
CHURCH I FYFFE CULVERDEN CULLENSWOOD ROSE GLEN SEATTLE TALLAGEIRA MAL
LENSTEH BOOTHARH YUNNDAGA GLEN IRIS MULLENDEREE THEBARTON WHITEM
WEST GROVE PURLEY WILLIAMSFORD BAW BAW BULGANDRY MINSTER PORTHCAWL GUN
OOLABRAR MISIDA WELLS PEYIA KEPSAU ANGAS DAW PARK OSWALD
FAR AS SUDBROOKE TABER DUNDONNELL TUMBULGUM KILARA
HUT MOUNT MARGARET EARLY RISE DAVISTOWN BADAI NORTH WILLAMSTOWN
LEVUE HI L ELWOOD MOUNT COMPASS PATHHEAD YAKAHAMA GLENROI HEIG
ILGA LLANERFYL SILVERHOPE PUKEMIRO JUNC PIRONGIA BENE ASHLEWORT
HAN IKIRO BENANEE BANGAL KNORRIT FLAT MARENGA DALMATIA MORRIS
MAXWELLTOWN BUTLER FIFA LAKEWOOD HAVRA SURRY
SALT BUSH BRIMIN ITALIAN GULLY PINE PARK WARRAH CREEK STAUNTON SPRI
UTRECHT ROSSVALE BANDIANA BULIMBA GLEN HEATHER TOWER WA
H TATONGA DOWNER ALLON COORABIE KIRKWALL BOWSER CHARLEVILLE CALENDAR
MORENDAH MOUNT DARLING HIGHTON BARRAPOORT CORRYTON DYMOCK
CAWTRY TERRAGONG HURDLE FLAT DALSWINTON SAINT RUDEAUX KOTARI CE

Australian Pavilion

Expo 2005 Aichi Japan

Reinforcing connections between Japan and Australia, the design of the Pavilion is developed from the Expo theme of "Nature's Wisdom / Nature's Matrix" and presents the nation as a contemporary place of sophistication, complexity and depth.

The entire Pavilion is in the form of an open Matrix, a complex three dimensional construction of repeated rectangular modules. The building becomes an inside-out structure, open to Japan and to the world, a seemingly endless unfolding of space and surface, accommodating display graphics, showcases and multimedia. At the centre of the building, the Matrix is opened out to form a celebration space, a multipurpose area for live entertainment and trade gatherings. The Matrix would be formed of surfaces and textures both virtual and real, with spaces for experimental installations and temporary displays. It would be entirely prefabricated in Australia, and shipped to Japan for fast and economical erection.

Externally, a glass-enclosed swimming pool forms an event icon, reflecting the Pavilion's display theme of water, where the interior is a progression through Australia environments from dry inland to wet coast, all based on the theme of water as a resource and natural element.

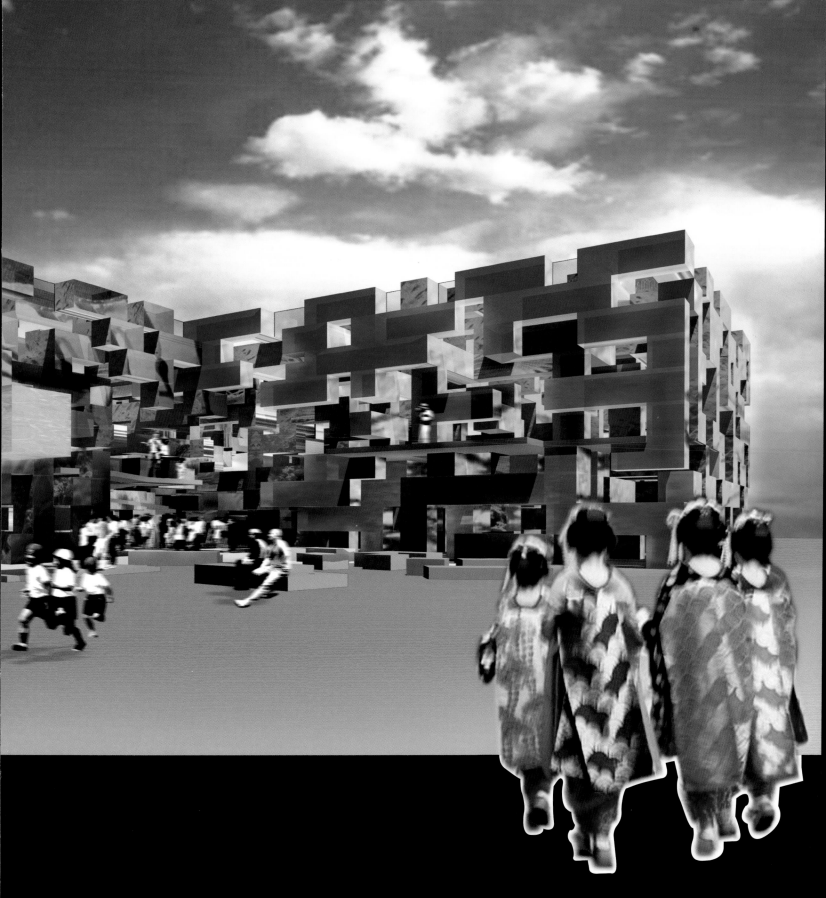

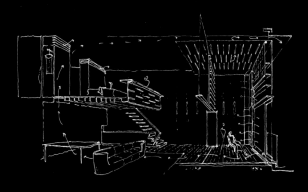

Portico

Scots Church Redevelopment
Sydney
2000–2005

left
Section of a typical two-storey apartment, showing the natural ventilation system and the glass-enclosed wintergarden.

below left
Typical floor plan.

bottom
West elevation.

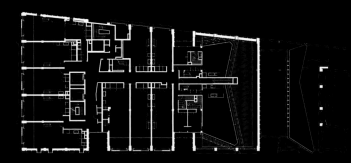

Won as a result of a limited competition, this project explores the redevelopment of the disused heritage-listed 1920s Scots Church in Sydney's CBD. Currently under construction, the project involves the conversion of the former church building and its airspace into residential units with some commercial uses at the lower levels. A stratum containing the original church auditorium of 2500 seats is to be retained by the Church and restored.

The six level heritage building was originally designed to have an additional 12 floors. During the Depression of the 1930s this scheme was abandoned, but the new development utilises the original support structure and references the neo- Gothic massing of the original proposal.

To achieve a maximum number of premium apartments, a system of two-level units was developed with corridors and lift access at every second floor. The whole building is within a sloping height-limit plane, which preserves solar access to Wynyard Park, south of the site. The elevation created by the sequence of double-storey apartment boxes continues the proportions of the Perpendicular Gothic façade below, emphasising the building's verticality and silhouette.

Sculptural roof forms are developed as a series of sky follies leaning over each of the rectilinear 'towers', with the northernmost looking towards the Harbour. The façade of the double storey apartments augments views to the sky and the city, and integrates natural ventilation through the use of operable sliding doors and shading elements. The attached wintergardens function as an acoustic buffer and a passive solar warming system to allow daylight to penetrate deep into the apartments. Ceiling plenums and thermal 'chimneys' on the wintergarden façades serve as a natural cross ventilation system, reducing air-conditioning requirements for the apartments.

The tower forms of the new building utilize sandstone colours to relate with the restored stone base, as well as expanses of seamed zinc and glazing. The interplay of solid and light, zinc and glass, combined with the irregular rhythm of coloured glazing panels, blinds and shutters, creates an urban elevation that reflects both its residential use and its relationship to the heritage building below.

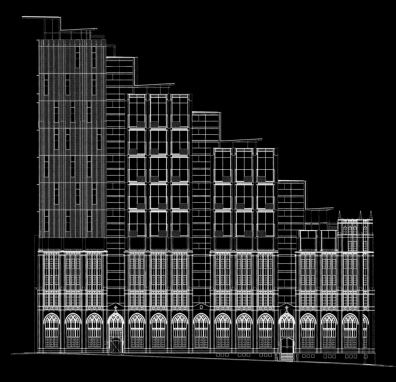

Atria

Clarence Street Residential Tower
Sydney
2002–2006

Located on an irregular city block, the Atria (won in competition) has been designed with 106 apartments over 25 levels. Ground floor tenancy spaces and a public garden link Clarence and Kent Streets.

The project, currently in development, has been designed as a tower and low-rise podium. The podium retains the warehouse character of its mid-town location with stacked two storey high apartments, whilst the tower responds to the various aspects of the void spaces surrounding the site. The brick and glass podium façade relates to Clarence Street, and the western copper-clad façade establishes a relationship with the heritage warehouses of Kent Street.

The defining element of the plan is the 'Ravine', a full height open space that runs through the entire section of the building providing northern sun, and city and harbour views, for many of the apartments. This tall void is open on one side above the adjoining heritage building and negates the sense of enclosure generated by the restricted urban site. The base of the 'Ravine' will be heavily planted and a major public artwork is planned.

Horizontal breaks in the building section define a change in plan, and provide mid level roof terraces, which allow light and air movement to penetrate to the centre of the site. Private glazed 'wintergarden' balconies provide a high level of thermal and acoustic control for the building's occupants.

The tower will be clad in heavily patterned precast concrete, the steel moulds for which will become an installation in the apartment tower foyer. Other external surfaces will be solar and white glass, articulated with shaped zinc fins.

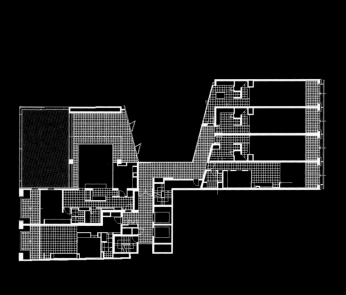

above
Typical apartment plan.

right
Glass wintergardens screen
the Clarence Street apartment
façades.

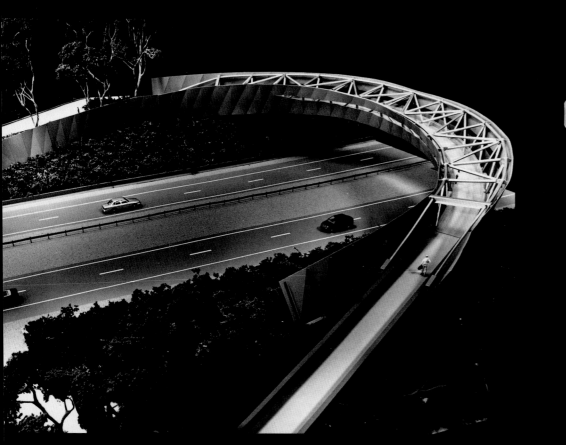

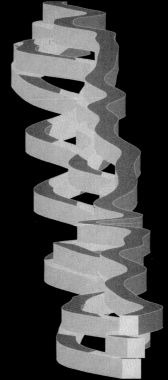

above
Model of the pedestrian
bridge, formed from the
sweep of the sound walls over
the road. It encloses the
motorist's first view of the
Melbourne skyline.

above right
Telephoto rendering of gabion
structures for earth berm
sound walls at the northern
end of the freeway.

right
The sound walls under
construction.

Craigieburn Bypass

Hume Freeway
Melbourne
2000–2004

Sound walls and 'road furniture' for a new 32km stretch of freeway linking the Hume Highway with the Melbourne Ring Road were designed in association with Landscape Architects Taylor Cullity Lethlean. Artist and sculptor Robert Owen has also been creatively involved in the concept design and modelling of all of the elements.

Currently under construction, the project has been designed to be experienced at a freeway speed of 110 km per hour. It includes three series of sculptural sound walls, a pedestrian bridge and a set of design parameters for road bridges, crash barriers and retaining structures.

The main series of walls (by Tonkin Zulaikha Greer) total over 2 kilometres in length, and are made from facetted austenitic steel sheets modelled in simple concave and convex folds to produce a gently undulating wave of steel floating on a recessed dark concrete base.

A second series of walls, by Taylor Cullity Lethlean, are to be translucent and transparent, preserving light and views from residential areas. These are edge-lit acrylic, sandblasted with a digital pattern and overlaid with coloured precast concrete blades,which form a relationship with the existing Melbourne Portal by architects Denton Corker Marshall. The third series, by Tonkin Zulaikha Greer, builds on the existing landform with dramatic earth sculpting. The use of gabions and heavily planted earth berms will achieve the required sound control.

A major element of the work is a new pedestrian bridge, which has been designed as a gateway to the distant city of Melbourne, visible on the horizon. The bridge, a complex curve in plan and elevation, is a tubular steel truss faced with the same austenitic steel as the main sound walls, which at this point appear to leap over the road in a gesture of welcome or farewell.

Contemporary Performing Arts Centre
Redfern
2003–2006

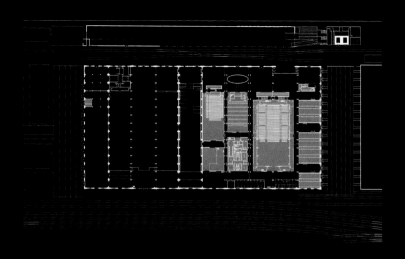

The **Contemporary Performing Arts Centre** is located in the 1880s Carriage Works of the disused Eveleigh Rail Yards in Sydney's inner west. It is the first stage in a new creative arts precinct that is to include both cultural and residential components. The Eveleigh Carriage Works is one of a pair of buildings; the other, the Locomotive Workshop, is located on the southern side of the railway and has been converted as technology research and office space.

The former Carriage Works is a long 19th Century brick 'shed' with repetitive iron-framed gabled bays. Carriages were built and repaired here for over a century, and the building retains its original built fabric and industrial atmosphere.

To accommodate professional and emerging contemporary performance-based artists, the project proposes three large flexible theatres, together with rehearsal spaces, workshops and an administration centre, all housed in discrete new forms. The foyers and public areas occupy the voids between these forms, permitting long vistas across the original space. This non-hierarchical planning strategy contrasts with the hierarchical space of the conventional theatre.

The principal Performance Space has been designed for experimental and acrobatic theatre, and requires the removal of a portion of the original iron and steel roof to increase the height of the theatre. The new roof, modulated to the scale of the existing gabled roof, will become an internally lit beacon. The old trusses will be reused as a gateway structure at the entrance to the complex. Open-plan foyers and other spaces will retain their original patinated heritage structures, while the new forms – platforms and boxes – will be clear modern insertions into this 'free space'.

above
Ground floor plan.

right
The foyer extends the full width of the Centre.

54

Foyer detail

left
The Small Performance Space

Award listing

National Trust NSW Heritage Award – Built Work Category	2002
Sir Henry Parkes Memorial School of Arts Tenterfield	
RAIA Merit Award for the Killcare House, with Ellen Woolley, Architect	2001
RAIA Merit Award for Urban Design for the Homebush Masterplan	2000
RAIA Merit Award Commendation for Conservation of Customs House with Jackson Teece Chesterman Willis	
RAIA Environment Award for Olympic Plaza Lighting Towers	
International RICS Award for Olympic Plaza Lighting Towers	
Institute of Lighting Engineers Grand Merit Award for Olympic Plaza Lighting Towers	
RAIA National President's Award for Recycled Buildings for Casula Powerhouse	1999
RAIA Merit Award for Recycled Buildings for Casula Powerhouse	
RAIA National Access Citation Award for Casula Powerhouse	
Property Council NSW 'Development of the Year' for Customs House	
ACEA Engineering Excellence Award for Olympic Plaza Lighting Towers	
Boral Timber Award for Excellence in Timber for Whale Beach House	
RAIA Merit Award for Affordable Housing with Roderick Simpson Architect	1996
National RAIA Environment Award for Affordable Housing	
RAIA National Walter Burley Griffin Award for Urban Design for Rocks Square	1994
NSW Chapter Merit Award for Urban Design for Rocks Square	
Boral Award for Excellence in Timber for Rocks Square	
RAIA Merit Award for National Memorial to the Australian Vietnam Forces	1993
Concrete Institute of Australia Merit Award for National Memorial to the Australian Vietnam Forces	
Master Builders Association Merit Award for National Memorial to the Australian Vietnam Forces	
Metal Building Award for Royal Blind Society Library Services Building	
RAIA Greenaway Award for conservation for the Hyde Park Barracks Museum	1992
RAIA National Lachlan Macquarie Award for conservation for the Hyde Park Barracks Museum	
RAIA Merit Award for Royal Blind Society Library Services Building	1991
RAIA Merit Award for Overseas Passenger Terminal, Lawrence Nield and Partners and NSW Dept of Public Works Government Architects Branch	1988
RAIA Lloyd Rees Urban Design Award for the Circular Quay Project, NSW Dept of Public Works Government Architects Branch	

ACKNOWLEDGMENTS

All photography © Patrick Bingham-Hall
except as listed below:

© Fretwell Photography – 26, 27
© Scott Frances – 36, 38 left, 40 above, 40 below
© John Gollings – 42 top, 42 below, 43, 53, 54, 55, 158
© Bart Maiorana – 44, 45, 46, 47 top, 47 below, 65 above,
    65 below, 67, 68, 70 above, 81, 133 above
© Assassi – 60, 61
© Eric Seirins – 62 left, 62 right, 63
© Manoel Nunes – 91
© Seewald-Hagen – 93
© Neil Mackenzie – 116
© Richard Glover – 124, 125 above, 125 below

All drawings and digital illustrations © Tonkin Zulaikha Greer
except as listed below:

© Ken Unsworth – 48
© Multiplex – 151

Endpapers: A list of most of the people who have worked
with TZG on these projects. We thank them all.

BEN PAK-POY JANE PALMER MANO PONNAMBALAM BRUCE PRESTON JOHN PRITCHARD HEIDI PRONK GERARD REINMUTH ANGELA RHEINLAENDER TRUDY RICK
INE STEPHEN VARADY JASON VEALE KON VOURTOUMIS JOANNA VRANISTAS ELIZABETH WEARNE GEORGIA WEBB JULIAN WONG PATRICK WONG ELLEN WOOLLEY VICTOR YO
CUTHBERT MATTHEW DARWON SCOTT DAVIS TRINA DAY SCOTT FALVEY TORSTEN FIEDLER CHRISTIAN FISHER MIRIAM FITZPATRICK KERRY GALLAGHER CLAIRE GILLIS YANN
JDSON JEREMY HUGHES HELEN HUGHES TSE HUI THE BASIT HUSSAIN TOM ISAKSSON BEN JOHNSON TAISSA KANG AMELIA KELLY KAREN KENNEDY IVANKA KOPROVIC FRA
USE MICHAEL MORGAN MARCIA MORLEY RICHARD MOULAY ELIZABETH MUIR LISA MULLAN ETAI NAVON ANDREW NIMMO CLAUDIA NOVATI DARRAGH O'BRIEN CHRISTIAN OL
RICKARD WOLFGANG RIPBERGER PAUL ROLFE JULIA SCHILLING BETTINA SIEGMUND JEN SMIT ARI TAHA TONY TAUSSIG ANNE TAYLOR TOM ISAKSSON LYDIA TIUTIUNNIK PE
YOUNG BRIAN ZULAIKHA OSCAR ANDREAZZA LIZ BOWRA PHILLIP BURCHMORE BARBARA BURGESS LARRY BURNETT JOHN CHESTERMAN REBECCA CLEAVES ANDREW COR
ANNICK GOLDSMITH JAMES GRANT TIM GREER LINDA GREGORIOU BYRON HARFORD ALEX HAW RICHARD HEALEY-FINLAY NICK HEBDEN AMELIA HOLLIDAY SOPHIE HOPP
C FRANK LE PETIT RUTH LEIMINER SCOTT LESTER MARGARET LIU GUY LUSCOMBE JAN LY JULIE MACKENZIE NEIL MACKENZIE SANDRA MARSHALL KIEREN MCINERNEY MAR
AN OLIVER ROGER O'SULLIVAN REINFRIED OTTER BEN PAK-POY JANE PALMER MANO PONNAMBALAM BRUCE PRESTON JOHN PRITCHARD HEIDI PRONK GERARD REINMUTH
NIK PETER TONKIN LAURA VALLENTINE STEPHEN VARADY JASON VEALE KON VOURTOUMIS JOANNA VRANISTAS ELIZABETH WEARNE GEORGIA WEBB JULIAN WONG PATRICK
CORBETT MELANIE CRICK DIRIMA CUTHBERT MATTHEW DARWON SCOTT DAVIS TRINA DAY SCOTT FALVEY TORSTEN FIEDLER CHRISTIAN FISHER MIRIAM FITZPATRICK KER
HOPPE KAREN HORNE MARY-ELLEN HUDSON JEREMY HUGHES HELEN HUGHES TSE HUI THE BASIT HUSSAIN TOM ISAKSSON BEN JOHNSON TAISSA KANG AMELIA KELLY K
NEY MARY MONAGLE ANTHONY MOORHOUSE MICHAEL MORGAN MARCIA MORLEY RICHARD MOULAY ELIZABETH MUIR LISA MULLAN ETAI NAVON ANDREW NIMMO CLAUDIA
REINMUTH ANGELA RHEINLAENDER TRUDY RICKARD WOLFGANG RIPBERGER PAUL ROLFE JULIA SCHILLING BETTINA SIEGMUND JEN SMIT ARI TAHA TONY TAUSSIG ANNE
WONG PATRICK WONG ELLEN WOOLLEY VICTOR YOUNG BRIAN ZULAIKHA OSCAR ANDREAZZA LIZ BOWRA PHILLIP BURCHMORE BARBARA BURGESS LARRY BURNETT JOHN
FITZPATRICK KERRY GALLAGHER CLAIRE GILLIS YANNICK GOLDSMITH JAMES GRANT TIM GREER LINDA GREGORIOU BYRON HARFORD ALEX HAW RICHARD HEALEY-FINLAY
ELIA KELLY KAREN KENNEDY IVANKA KOPROVIC FRANK LE PETIT RUTH LEIMINER SCOTT LESTER MARGARET LIU GUY LUSCOMBE JAN LY JULIE MACKENZIE NEIL MACKENZIE
CLAUDIA NOVATI DARRAGH O'BRIEN CHRISTIAN OLIVER ROGER O'SULLIVAN REINFRIED OTTER BEN PAK-POY JANE PALMER MANO PONNAMBALAM BRUCE PRESTON JOHN
ANNE TAYLOR TOM ISAKSSON LYDIA TIUTIUNNIK PETER TONKIN LAURA VALLENTINE STEPHEN VARADY JASON VEALE KON VOURTOUMIS JOANNA VRANISTAS ELIZABETH W
JOHN CHESTERMAN REBECCA CLEAVES ANDREW CORBETT MELANIE CRICK DIRIMA CUTHBERT MATTHEW DARWON SCOTT DAVIS TRINA DAY SCOTT FALVEY TORSTEN FIED
FINLAY NICK HEBDEN AMELIA HOLLIDAY SOPHIE HOPPE KAREN HORNE MARY-ELLEN HUDSON JEREMY HUGHES HELEN HUGHES TSE HUI THE BASIT HUSSAIN TOM ISAKSSO
CKENZIE SANDRA MARSHALL KIEREN MCINERNEY MARY MONAGLE ANTHONY MOORHOUSE MICHAEL MORGAN MARCIA MORLEY RICHARD MOULAY ELIZABETH MUIR LISA MU
J JOHN PRITCHARD HEIDI PRONK GERARD REINMUTH ANGELA RHEINLAENDER TRUDY RICKARD WOLFGANG RIPBERGER PAUL ROLFE JULIA SCHILLING BETTINA SIEGMUND
TH WEARNE GEORGIA WEBB JULIAN WONG PATRICK WONG ELLEN WOOLLEY VICTOR YOUNG BRIAN ZULAIKHA OSCAR ANDREAZZA LIZ BOWRA PHILLIP BURCHMORE BARBARA
CHRISTIAN FISHER MIRIAM FITZPATRICK KERRY GALLAGHER CLAIRE GILLIS YANNICK GOLDSMITH JAMES GRANT TIM GREER LINDA GREGORIOU BYRON HARFORD ALEX
N BEN JOHNSON TAISSA KANG AMELIA KELLY KAREN KENNEDY IVANKA KOPROVIC FRANK LE PETIT RUTH LEIMINER SCOTT LESTER MARGARET LIU GUY LUSCOMBE JAN LY J
LLAN ETAI NAVON ANDREW NIMMO CLAUDIA NOVATI DARRAGH O'BRIEN CHRISTIAN OLIVER ROGER O'SULLIVAN REINFRIED OTTER BEN PAK-POY JANE PALMER MANO PON
ND JEN SMIT ARI TAHA TONY TAUSSIG ANNE TAYLOR TOM ISAKSSON LYDIA TIUTIUNNIK PETER TONKIN LAURA VALLENTINE STEPHEN VARADY JASON VEALE KON VOURTOUMIS
A BURGESS LARRY BURNETT JOHN CHESTERMAN REBECCA CLEAVES ANDREW CORBETT MELANIE CRICK DIRIMA CUTHBERT MATTHEW DARWON SCOTT DAVIS TRINA DAY SCOT
W RICHARD HEALEY-FINLAY NICK HEBDEN AMELIA HOLLIDAY SOPHIE HOPPE KAREN HORNE MARY-ELLEN HUDSON JEREMY HUGHES HELEN HUGHES TSE HUI THE BASIT HU
MACKENZIE NEIL MACKENZIE SANDRA MARSHALL KIEREN MCINERNEY MARY MONAGLE ANTHONY MOORHOUSE MICHAEL MORGAN MARCIA MORLEY RICHARD MOULAY ELI
BALAM BRUCE PRESTON JOHN PRITCHARD HEIDI PRONK GERARD REINMUTH ANGELA RHEINLAENDER TRUDY RICKARD WOLFGANG RIPBERGER PAUL ROLFE JULIA SCHILLING
VRANISTAS ELIZABETH WEARNE GEORGIA WEBB JULIAN WONG PATRICK WONG ELLEN WOOLLEY VICTOR YOUNG BRIAN ZULAIKHA OSCAR ANDREAZZA LIZ BOWRA PHILLIP B
ALVEY TORSTEN FIEDLER CHRISTIAN FISHER MIRIAM FITZPATRICK KERRY GALLAGHER CLAIRE GILLIS YANNICK GOLDSMITH JAMES GRANT TIM GREER LINDA GREGORIOU
USSAIN TOM ISAKSSON BEN JOHNSON TAISSA KANG AMELIA KELLY KAREN KENNEDY IVANKA KOPROVIC FRANK LE PETIT RUTH LEIMINER SCOTT LESTER MARGARET LIU
ELIZABETH MUIR LISA MULLAN ETAI NAVON ANDREW NIMMO CLAUDIA NOVATI DARRAGH O'BRIEN CHRISTIAN OLIVER ROGER O'SULLIVAN REINFRIED OTTER BEN PAK-PO
CHILLING BETTINA SIEGMUND JEN SMIT ARI TAHA TONY TAUSSIG ANNE TAYLOR TOM ISAKSSON LYDIA TIUTIUNNIK PETER TONKIN LAURA VALLENTINE STEPHEN VARADY JA
RA PHILLIP BURCHMORE BARBARA BURGESS LARRY BURNETT JOHN CHESTERMAN REBECCA CLEAVES ANDREW CORBETT MELANIE CRICK DIRIMA CUTHBERT MATTHEW DAR
REGORIOU BYRON HARFORD ALEX HAW RICHARD HEALEY-FINLAY NICK HEBDEN AMELIA HOLLIDAY SOPHIE HOPPE KAREN HORNE MARY-ELLEN HUDSON JEREMY HUGHES H
ET LIU GUY LUSCOMBE JAN LY JULIE MACKENZIE NEIL MACKENZIE SANDRA MARSHALL KIEREN MCINERNEY MARY MONAGLE ANTHONY MOORHOUSE MICHAEL MORGAN MA
POY JANE PALMER MANO PONNAMBALAM BRUCE PRESTON JOHN PRITCHARD HEIDI PRONK GERARD REINMUTH ANGELA RHEINLAENDER TRUDY RICKARD WOLFGANG RIPP
JASON VEALE KON VOURTOUMIS JOANNA VRANISTAS ELIZABETH WEARNE GEORGIA WEBB JULIAN WONG PATRICK WONG ELLEN WOOLLEY VICTOR YOUNG BRIAN ZULAIKHA
W DARWON SCOTT DAVIS TRINA DAY SCOTT FALVEY TORSTEN FIEDLER CHRISTIAN FISHER MIRIAM FITZPATRICK KERRY GALLAGHER CLAIRE GILLIS YANNICK GOLDSMITH JAM
HELEN HUGHES TSE HUI THE BASIT HUSSAIN TOM ISAKSSON BEN JOHNSON TAISSA KANG AMELIA KELLY KAREN KENNEDY IVANKA KOPROVIC FRANK LE PETIT RUTH LEIM
MARCIA MORLEY RICHARD MOULAY ELIZABETH MUIR LISA MULLAN ETAI NAVON ANDREW NIMMO CLAUDIA NOVATI DARRAGH O'BRIEN CHRISTIAN OLIVER ROGER O'SULL
NG RIPBERGER PAUL ROLFE JULIA SCHILLING BETTINA SIEGMUND JEN SMIT ARI TAHA TONY TAUSSIG ANNE TAYLOR TOM ISAKSSON LYDIA TIUTIUNNIK PETER TONKIN LAU
JLAIKHA OSCAR ANDREAZZA LIZ BOWRA PHILLIP BURCHMORE BARBARA BURGESS LARRY BURNETT JOHN CHESTERMAN REBECCA CLEAVES ANDREW CORBETT MELANIE C
TH JAMES GRANT TIM GREER LINDA GREGORIOU BYRON HARFORD ALEX HAW RICHARD HEALEY-FINLAY NICK HEBDEN AMELIA HOLLIDAY SOPHIE HOPPE KAREN HORNE MA
TH LEIMINER SCOTT LESTER MARGARET LIU GUY LUSCOMBE JAN LY JULIE MACKENZIE NEIL MACKENZIE SANDRA MARSHALL KIEREN MCINERNEY MARY MONAGLE ANTHON
'SULLIVAN REINFRIED OTTER BEN PAK-POY JANE PALMER MANO PONNAMBALAM BRUCE PRESTON JOHN PRITCHARD HEIDI PRONK GERARD REINMUTH ANGELA RHEINLAE
LAURA VALLENTINE STEPHEN VARADY JASON VEALE KON VOURTOUMIS JOANNA VRANISTAS ELIZABETH WEARNE GEORGIA WEBB JULIAN WONG PATRICK WONG ELLEN WOO
CRICK DIRIMA CUTHBERT MATTHEW DARWON SCOTT DAVIS TRINA DAY SCOTT FALVEY TORSTEN FIEDLER CHRISTIAN FISHER MIRIAM FITZPATRICK KERRY GALLAGHER CLAI
MARY-ELLEN HUDSON JEREMY HUGHES HELEN HUGHES TSE HUI THE BASIT HUSSAIN TOM ISAKSSON BEN JOHNSON TAISSA KANG AMELIA KELLY KAREN KENNEDY IVANKA KO
MOORHOUSE MICHAEL MORGAN MARCIA MORLEY RICHARD MOULAY ELIZABETH MUIR LISA MULLAN ETAI NAVON ANDREW NIMMO CLAUDIA NOVATI DARRAGH O'BRIEN C
ENDER TRUDY RICKARD WOLFGANG RIPBERGER PAUL ROLFE JULIA SCHILLING BETTINA SIEGMUND JEN SMIT ARI TAHA TONY TAUSSIG ANNE TAYLOR TOM ISAKSSON LYDI
OOLLEY VICTOR YOUNG BRIAN ZULAIKHA OSCAR ANDREAZZA LIZ BOWRA PHILLIP BURCHMORE BARBARA BURGESS LARRY BURNETT JOHN CHESTERMAN REBECCA CLEA
NER CLAIRE GILLIS YANNICK GOLDSMITH JAMES GRANT TIM GREER LINDA GREGORIOU BYRON HARFORD ALEX HAW RICHARD HEALEY-FINLAY NICK HEBDEN AMELIA HOLLI
IVANKA KOPROVIC FRANK LE PETIT RUTH LEIMINER SCOTT LESTER MARGARET LIU GUY LUSCOMBE JAN LY JULIE MACKENZIE NEIL MACKENZIE SANDRA MARSHALL KIERE
H O'BRIEN CHRISTIAN OLIVER ROGER O'SULLIVAN REINFRIED OTTER BEN PAK-POY JANE PALMER MANO PONNAMBALAM BRUCE PRESTON JOHN PRITCHARD HEIDI PRONK
KSSON LYDIA TIUTIUNNIK PETER TONKIN LAURA VALLENTINE STEPHEN VARADY JASON VEALE KON VOURTOUMIS JOANNA VRANISTAS ELIZABETH WEARNE GEORGIA WEBB JU
CLEAVES ANDREW CORBETT MELANIE CRICK DIRIMA CUTHBERT MATTHEW DARWON SCOTT DAVIS TRINA DAY SCOTT FALVEY TORSTEN FIEDLER CHRISTIAN FISHER MIRIA
HOLLIDAY SOPHIE HOPPE KAREN HORNE MARY-ELLEN HUDSON JEREMY HUGHES HELEN HUGHES TSE HUI THE BASIT HUSSAIN TOM ISAKSSON BEN JOHNSON TAISSA KA